the
BOLLYWOOD
Cookbook

the BOLLYWOOD *Cookbook*

The glamorous world of the actors and over 75 of their favorite recipes

Bulbul Mankani

Kyle Books

For my mother, Kanta Mankani, with love and gratitude

This book owes its coming together to many people who reached out and helped: Ravi Gupta at Mukta Arts, Vishal Patel at Dharma Productions, Rakeysh Mehra, Chitra Palekar, Suguna Sundaram, Sheena Sippy, Natasha Wade, Menaka Thadani, Aditi Mittal, Anjali Bhushan, Vijaya Dewan, Archana Singh, Mandira Shukla, Vaishali Banerjee, Deepika Deshpande Amin, Nandini Gulati and Deepti Naval.

I am truly grateful to my publishers, Bipin Shah, Kyle Cathie and Florentine Schwabbauer, for the support they extended at the worst moments, and to Diana Romany for editing the book.

This paperback edition published 2008

First published simultaneously in 2006 in Great Britain by Kyle Cathie Limited, in Germany by Christian Verlag GmbH and in India by Mapin Publishing.
Published in collaboration with National Book Trust, India

Kyle Cathie Limited
122 Arlington Road, London NW1 7HP
www.kylecathie.com

ISBN: 978-185626-765-6

Copyright © 2006 Christian Verlag GmbH, Germany
English Language Edition © 2006 Kyle Cathie Limited
Food Photography © 2006 Lisa Linder

A Cataloguing in Publication record for this title is available from the British Library.

Colour reproduction by Chromagraphics
Printed in Slovenia by MKT PRINT

Concept: Florentine Schwabbauer and Bulbul Mankani
Text: Bulbul Mankani
Brilliant Food Photographer: Lisa Linder
Brilliant Food Stylist: Linda Tubby
Picture Research: Mapin Publishing, India
Research and Supervision: Mapin Publishing, India
Design: pinkstripedesign.com
Assistant Editor: Georgina Atsiaris
Production: Sha Huxtable and Alice Holloway

Bulbul Mankani is hereby identified as the author of this work in accordance with Section 77 of the Copyright, Designs and Patents Act 1988.

Photograph Credits: pages 3 (right), 6 UTV; 3 (left), 9, 11, 68, 69, 72, 73, 74–75, 106, 113 (right) 117, 121, 131, 132, 137, 143 Mukta Arts; 7, 15, 24, 25, 43, 48–49, 146, 150 Dharma Productions; 10, 142 Rakeysh Mehra; 12–13 Ramesh Sippy Entertainment; 16–17 Vikram Bawa for *Cine Blitz*; 18, 19 UTV/Ashutosh Gowarikar Productions; 20, 83 Subi Samuel; 27, 42, 44, 66, 125 Dabboo Ratnani; 32 Rakesh Shreshta for Vikram Phadnis; 34 Jagdish Maali; 46 Sheena Sippy; 51, 168, 169 Sippy Films; 52 Atul Kasbekar for *Xylys*; 56 Atul Kasbekar; 53 Jhamu Sughand; 61, 120 Bulbul Mankani; 77, 162 (top), 170, 159 R.K. Films; 78, 79 Joy Datta; 89 Vikram Bawa; 93, 94 Vinod Chopra Productions; 97, 100 Rakeysh Om Prakash Mehra Productions; 107 Tanvir Ahmed; 105 Red Chillies; 113 (left) Filmkraft; 139 Raveena Tandon; 147, 149 Rakesh Shreshta; 156 Imperial Movietone; 157 R Shantaram; 158 Mehboob Khan; 160, 161 Chandra Barot; 162 (bottom), 166 Guru Dutt; 163 Navketan Films; 164–165 K Asif; 167 Kamaal Amrohi; 171 Muzaffar Ali

Contents

FOREWORD

The world can be divided into two kinds of people—those who eat to live and those who live to eat. It's the latter who add wonder, excitement, and adventure to their lives. These are the people who are willing to take chances with tastes and flavors, often making serendipitous discoveries, ranging from the humble and home-grown to the exotic and rare. They are always mindful and sensitive to their palates and olfactory responses, recognizing subtle differences in fragrance, flavor, texture, and taste, concerned equally with the quality of cuisine and its esthetic appeal.

Cooking is high art. The chef is not only an artist, he or she is also a magician conjuring up recipes based on both rational and intuitive knowledge of vegetables, fruit, fish, and seafood, meat and spices, and using a variety of cooking techniques. A great chef creates flavors both old and new.

Each country, each region, each society, and each community can be identified by their respective cuisine. The style of cuisine can tell you a great deal about the history of the people who created it. Even within the same cuisine, a dish will taste different when cooked by different cooks or households. No two chefs can produce the same dish with the same flavor. The difference lies in their attitude to food. For foodies, particularly those who also love to try their hand at cooking, there is nothing quite like trying out new and exciting recipes.

A new cookbook always comes with a promise of adventure. *The Bollywood Cookbook* is no exception. Everything about film stars is of perennial interest to their fans, including their culinary preferences. Unsurprisingly, most stars have chosen to offer recipes that are traditional to their community and region. A few have offered up recipes of dishes that they have learnt to enjoy. Leafing through this book, I notice that the favored cuisine of most film professionals is either tandoori or Mughal or the food that they have grown up with in their parents' home. Raveena Tandon favors Sai Bhaji and other Sindhi dishes while Shilpa Shetty shows a fondness for Bunt cooking from Mangalore, Rahul Bose has his Bengali recipes, and Deepti Naval her vegetarian Punjabi specialties like stuffed karela. Undoubtedly, the true gourmets (and gourmands) with a taste for a wide range of cuisines are members of the Kapoor clan. Having partaken of innumerable delectable meals at Shashi and Jennifer Kapoor's home and a couple of times at the late Raj Kapoor's fabulous parties, I know first-hand that they are more discerning of food than anyone else in the Mumbai film industry.

My own food tastes are fairly eclectic. I tend to favor classical Mughal cuisine and consider it by far the tastiest and most sophisticated anywhere. There are quite a number of great meals that I have had in different parts of the world, but I remember one meal in particular. It was the dinner that my film unit and I had organized to celebrate Shabana Azmi's birthday when we were shooting *Mandi* in Hyderabad way back in 1982. We managed to find an old rheumy-eyed alcoholic of a khansama (cook) from the barkus (barracks), a neighborhood in the disused cantonment quarter of the erstwhile Nizam's army. He had the reputation of being the only cook who knew the original Hyderabadi recipe for a stuffed whole lamb (goat). Peering at me from behind his thick smoke-stained spectacles, he told me that he hadn't cooked it for over thirty years. If it did not come right, he was not to blame, he mumbled. He said it would take him twenty-four hours of cooking time and when it was ready we would have to eat it immediately to enjoy its fulsome flavors and the succulent texture of its meat. Soon after, he and his bawarchis (assistants) got to work. The whole process began about twenty-eight hours ahead of the dinner. The dressing and marination of the lamb was followed by the elaborate stuffing, consisting of chickens with hard-cooked eggs in them wrapped in a bed of flavored basmati supplemented by a great variety of dried fruit, nuts, and spices. All of this was sewn into the animal's cavity. The actual cooking took place in a clay-lined pit spread with live coals of tamarind wood. Rice husk, stalks, and assorted dry grasses were piled on top of the lamb and covered with another layer of wet clay. Exactly twenty-four hours later, the maestro dug up a stuffed lamb cooked to perfection. For accompaniments, we had Hyderabadi lagan ka gosht (mutton cooked with yogurt and peanuts), asafjahi korma (mutton cooked with almonds), and shikampuri kebabs (spicy meat kebabs stuffed with paneer), thanks to Shabana's Hyderabadi aunts. Various other condiments, rotis, and breads made up the rest of the meal. I will never forget that birthday of Shabana's. Every time I have a great Mughal meal I am immediately transported to that evening, a quarter of a century ago. Incidentally, I agree with Suneil Shetty's adage, "eat breakfast like a king, lunch like a prince and dine like a pauper." A great tip for good health.

For people who love food and for those who are curious about what their film heroes and heroines eat, this book is a joy. Try out the recipes; I am sure they'll be great. Enjoy!

Shyam Benegal

INSIDE BOLLYWOOD

Chamma Chamma baaje re meri painjaniyan
Tere paas aaun, teri saanson mein samaaon raja
Teri needein chura loon
Chamma chamma…

The sound of my anklets go jingle, jingle
I'll come close to you and take your breath away
I'll steal the sleep from your eyes…

—Song lyrics from *China Gate*, adapted in *Moulin Rouge*

Moulin Rouge, the 2001 musical featuring Nicole Kidman and directed by Baz Luhrmann, was inspired by his watching Bollywood films. It is a great Western representation of the form and charm of Bollywood. The simple love-centered plot with its extravagant songs and dances, and emotional tsunamis, all conveyed with wonderful melodrama and high pitch comedy, is quintessentially Bollywood.

Picture this: you are the only and much loved child of a wealthy industrialist family. Love walks into your carefree, fun-filled world in the guise of a poor, hardworking, self-respecting individual and you are swept away to picture-perfect lands. Together you express the poetry of your love in exquisitely synchronized music and dancing. As you plan your happily-ever-after, the world throws obstacles in your path. You and your lover successfully battle against adversity, leading to the climactic moment where all is set right and you walk hand in hand into the sunset. This is Bollyworld: the Bollywood masala that has sustained the collective imagination of India and Indian communities all around the world. The costumes are elaborate, the locations a catalog of impossible beauty, the songs and dances a triumph of cultural celebration.

Bollywood cinema creates an imaginary hyper-reality—immaculate sprawling bungalows, perfect weather where no heat or dust ever reaches, heroes with god-like skills and values, chaste and loyal women who look like goddesses every breathing moment. The magic is spun with wonderful deliberation, giving the viewer a ticket to temporary amnesia and a total liberation of their fantasies.

In the darkness of the theater Bollywood wants to submerge you in a myriad of emotions. Love, comedy, suspense, tragedy, horror, thrills, and spills engulf the audience as they watch, transfixed. The structure of the Bollywood film is key. It is usually between 150 to180 minutes long and is broken into two parts by an interval of ten minutes. The plot unfolds in a manner that ensures the interval comes at a climactic point in the story, keeping the audience on the edge of their seats. There are always subplots and flashbacks, stories within stories, and a multitude of conflicts and coincidences that lead the plot to its inevitable conclusion. These techniques are a tradition inherited from the two principal Indian epics, the *Mahabharat* and the *Ramayan*.

Since the 1990s, Bollywood has become more nostalgic, returning to traditional roots, karmic belief systems, and the importance of the family in society.

Parsi theater from Mumbai, the art of Ravi Varma, the nautanki (street theater), and many indigenous art forms have influenced Bollywood. In Sanskrit, the word for both dance and drama is *natya*, indicating the cultural bias for an affinity between theater and music. Bollywood is well known for its love of melodrama, though films have been toning down the pitch in recent years. The exaggerated acting and dialogue, the explosive nature of the background music score, the strength of passion, the full-force action sequences—all descend from theater. Despite this, the pace of Bollywood cinema is slow and expansive. It requires its viewers to be patient and the reward is a cathartic stretch of emotive power. The form and symbolism of Bollywood films will remain mysterious to a first-time viewer. But to those familiar with the films, it is a world set apart from reality and yet completely understood. It is this understanding, and the strong connection between audience and film, that has prevented too much experimentation in the past. Any change in form is slow to find acceptance.

above: Jackie Shroff in the role of a troubled and conflicted father in Subhash Ghai's *Yaadein* (2001).

Bollywood has crafted a convention that its audiences accept and participate in wholeheartedly. The rules are simple: love will always conquer; coincidence and divine providence are always at hand; brothers will meet on opposing sides of the law; parents will be disapproving; mothers and sisters will be doting and sacrificing; and the police force will blunder their way through the film but set everything right in the end. Silly maids, gardeners, fat relatives, and friends provide comic relief and vamps have hearts of gold. Justice will prevail even if only in the last reel of the film.

Bollywood has always been sensitive to the political and social climate of India. The political upheaval during the Emergency in the 1970s introduced themes of rebelliousness and individualism in films. The megastar of the '70s and '80s, Amitabh Bachchan, played heroes who challenged law and society and unleashed their anger and resentment against the world. Since

opposite page:
Aishwarya Rai got a new
raunchy look for the
'Ishq Kamina' song
sequence in *Shakti—The
Power* (2002). Here she is
seen in close-up looking like
a Maharastrian belle.

below: This sequence in
Rang De Basanti (2006)
got cut in the final film after
animal rights activist Menaka
Gandhi took objection.
However, the film went on
to become a big success.

the '90s, particularly with the increasing Indian diaspora around the world, Bollywood has become more nostalgic, returning to traditional roots, karmic belief systems, and the importance of the family in society.

Aditya Chopra, Sooraj Barjatya, and Karan Johar, the new generation of directors, have tuned into these desires and created heroes who look and talk in modern ways but whose hearts are rooted in tradition. Shah Rukh Khan, the biggest Bollywood star of today, plays characters that represent positive values of warmth, communication, love, and respect. He may look like a Western man but he carries his Indian heart on his sleeve.

New films are setting trends with their global feel. Their characters are comfortable in a foreign world but remain in touch with their roots through language and cultural values. While earlier films climaxed at the wedding scenes, more recent films go on to deal with issues after marriage. *Salaam Namaste* (2005), for example, is about a couple who live together as lovers, and its huge success indicates a change in the traditional mold. Characters in today's films have adapted to the modern world and have cemented a strong connection with their younger audience.

Modernity in Bollywood is slowly finding its way in. *Rang De Basanti*, a big success in 2006, is not a typical Hindi film. It entwines parallel stories of a group of freedom fighters struggling to free India from foreign rule, and the young protagonists attempting to expose corrupt politicians. The well-crafted script powerfully describes the journey that the characters undertake through the duration of the film. The songs sequences are not "set pieces," they flow more from the mood the film creates. The dialogues are natural and relaxed, the script isn't melodramatic, and the music and lyrics are distinctly modern.

Leading the brigade in the globalization of Bollywood, is the once Miss World and now premiere actress Aishwarya Rai, who has been on the cover of *Time Asia* magazine as the new face of Bollywood. She was the first Bollywood actress to make a bid in Hollywood, and her international presence is growing with appearances on shows like Oprah Winfrey and David Letterman, and her work in co-productions like *Bride and Prejudice* (2004), *Chaos* (2005), and *Provoked* (2006). Her Indian work has been prolific; her best films combine her extraordinary beauty with her wonderful dancing skills.

UTV MOTION PICTURES PRESENTS

RAKEYSH OMPRAKASH MEHRA'S
Rang De Basanti
a generation awakens

www.RangDeBasanti.net

Indian films have always been musical dramas and the songs and dances are intrinsic part of Bollywood. Indeed, elaborate song scripts are written and recorded very early in the film, usually over many days, even weeks. Songs have always sought to express the inner world of the characters. Expressing love physically was in the past, and today, taboo. Kissing, though allowed, immediately gives the film an adult certification, so physical desire is communicated instead through music. The lead actors tease, beckon, and playfully woo each other in melodious forms. In *Veer-Zaara* (2004), the lovers never touch each other except during a song sequence—it is the only medium through which they can express their passion. Dancing together is as intimate as Bollywood allows and the symbolism is now so ingrained that one does not expect to see physical intimacy. Art house films on the other hand have no songs or dances and are much less glamorous. They use realistic stories set in real locations and are told in more classical, Western terms. Art house film culture in Hindi is sparse today but had a distinct presence during the 1970s and '80s, spearheaded by films directed by Shyam Benegal.

The culture and reach of Bollywood songs is enormous and they can outlive the film by decades—a mediocre film can become a big success if the songs are popular. Bollywood film stars have become the pop star equivalents of the West, even though they only lip-sync to the voice of playback singers. International stage shows from Bollyworld are like pop concerts. The 2005 *Temptations* tour with Shah Rukh Khan had more than 25,000 people attending each show across the USA.

Indian films have always been musical dramas and the songs and dances are an intrinsic part of Bollywood. They have always sought to express the inner world of the characters.

The stories and themes of Indian films are simple but the stars themselves reach iconic status and can influence attitude, fashion, gestures, and speech in the everyday world. Aamir Khan once told a film festival audience of his days in school, when getting his hair to stay like his screen god Dev Anand's was far more absorbing than studies. Life has come a full circle for him. After he sported the short haircut for his role in *Dil Chahta Hai* (2001), every teenager copied it. Now, his longer hair in *Rang De Basanti* (2006) is the latest rage. Advertising, television shows, radio, and newspapers are driven by Bollywood through imagery, language, stylization, and content. With the subconscious deluge of all things Bollywood, the influence the stars hold is not surprising.

DHARMA PRODUCTIONS PRESENTS

KAL HO NAA HO

A STORY OF A LIFETIME... IN A HEARTBEAT

PRODUCED BY **YASH JOHAR** DIRECTED BY **NIKHIL ADVANI** WRITTEN BY **KARAN JOHAR** MUSIC BY **SHANKAR EHSAAN LOY** LYRICS BY **JAVED AKHTAR**

Sony Music www.khnhthefilm.com

कल हो ना हो

In an increasingly fractured and hostile world, film has become an essential and inevitable form of escapism. The retelling of the epics in modern ways is essential to Indians. It creates the web within which they understand their identity. Bollywood is multi-cultural in the Indian context and effortlessly integrates the regional ethnic divides. For years the charms of Bollywood have attracted audiences in the Middle East and parts of Africa. Now the Western world is also tuning in and responding with interest. The visual culture and exuberance of Bollywood is infectious—and the west is catching the fever and swaying in delight to its music!

Cinema and food are India's enduring passions. The flavors enliven our palates as much as the stars fill our imagination. The ethnic variations of our cuisine are unmatched and the tastes fiery and fantastic. Dive into the pages ahead and you will discover a diverse range of dishes from all over India, shared by the Bollywood stars themselves. Their recipes are inspiring and exciting and will create a slice of Bollywood magic in your very own home.

Savor the food fiesta, Bollywood ishtyle!

above: *Kal Ho Naa Ho* (2003) depicts a miniature India residing in New York. Its emotional rainbow is brought forth by the sunny Shah Rukh Khan spreading joy and cheer.

previous page: Abhishek Bachchan and Priyanka Chopra share a romantic moment in *Bluffmaster* (2006), a fun caper about a smart conman and his protégée.

above: The best of Bollywood in a photograph that took many weeks to come together. The photographer, Vikram Bawa, created this historic image featuring (from left to right): Aishwarya Rai, Amitabh Bachchan, Shah Rukh Khan, Akshay Kumar, Preity Zinta, Hrithik Roshan, Ajay Devgan, Viveik Oberoi, Sushmita Sen, Saif Ali Khan, and Bipasha Basu.

At forty, Shah Rukh Khan is the biggest star in Bollywood by sheer strength of his popularity across the world. The Indian diaspora and the Bollywood-loving universe are mesmerized by his emotive abilities, and the roles he plays continue to challenge him so that his superstar status only increases. *Kal Ho Naa Ho* (2003), is a perfect example of his connection with audiences. His character knows he is dying and chooses to bring cheer, romance, and song into the lives of the people he encounters. He can see through their frailties and gives them confidence and hope. Shah Rukh Khan plays the character effortlessly, and this is where his success is centered—he is the regular guy with a good heart who can be trusted to do the right thing at all times. In our increasingly fragmented times, he is a hero and role model.

Shah Rukh Khan

The range of emotions that Shah Rukh can convey, the high energetic youthful persona he can assume, the exuberance of his physical presence on screen and the sometimes naughty, sometimes pensive, and often loving expressions in his eyes are possibly what keep his huge audience hooked and asking for more—he makes you believe in the impossible. His career has taken him to the point where he is the absolute king. While he works with many big stars in his films, it is his name that continues to attract audiences.

His journey began in a simple middle class Delhi home where he spent a happy and loving childhood, went to one of the best schools and joined TAG, Barry John's theater group. One of his TAG mates recalls those days: "When everyone was pasting Aamir Khan and Salman Khan posters on their cupboards, it was unimaginable that our Shah Rukh would one day be the biggest icon!" His move to Mumbai after a few television serials introduced him to films. *Raju Ban Gaya Gentleman* (1992) was his first success. He was open to playing dark roles: the obsessive lover in *Darr* (1993) and the ruthless killer and vengeful strategist in *Baazigar* (1993). It is a gamble that payed off as they were well-crafted and very successful films and gave him the opportunity to exhibit his wide ranging skills.

For the younger generation of directors, he was the first choice to play the quintessential romantic hero. Both Aditya Chopra and later Karan Johar hit the right notes with their respective films *Dilwale Dulhaniya Le Jayenge* (1995) and

opposite page and right: Shah Rukh Khan captures the joy of coming back home. *Swades* (2004), touched a chord for many Indians who make the journey back to their country in order to create a positive future.

Kuch Kuch Hota Hai (1998). His vulnerable characters carried a romantic edge and represented the aspirations of the youth in the 90s. The media emphasized this by associating him with popular youth brands. Shah Rukh is the man of the masses, the darling of teenagers, and an icon for all.

Shah Rukh set up his own production company to allow him greater freedom to experiment with themes and roles (*Phir Bhi Dil Hai Hindustani* in 2000 and *Asoka* in 2001) although it was not easy to break out of the stereotypical image that he is so famous for and that has come to define him. But it is clear when you hear him speak that he has a sharp, articulate mind and a down-to-earth nature. During an interview on a TV show, he described himself as a bhand (street performer)—you can ask him to do anything, for the right price.

His passion for his work is immense and admirable. Despite a painful spinal problem he thrives on putting in long hours on set. He is currently working on the remake of *Don*, in which he plays the role originally made famous by another superstar, Amitabh Bachchan. When they worked together some years back in *Mohabbatein*, it was almost as if the superstar mantle was passed on by the legend to the next in line. And at the moment, King Khan rules.

Lamb Galouti

3½lbs lamb finely ground
11oz lamb fat (ask your butcher to give
   this to you)
2½oz ginger paste (see page 155)
2½oz garlic paste (see page 155)
5oz browned onion paste
¾oz red chili powder
1½oz roasted gram dal
   (chana dal)
¾oz garam masala (see page 154)
½oz awadhi masala (see page 154)
2 tablespoons saffron water
2 tablespoons kewra water
1 teaspoon clove powder
1 tablespoon ghee (see page 155)
sprigs of mint, to garnish
salt to taste

serves 6

A great specialty of Lucknow cuisine, this sumptuous kebab recipe comes from Jitendra Kumar, the chef of The Taj Land's End. Their restaurant, Masala Bay, hosts many dinners for the Khan family and they have provided a selection of his favorite dishes.

In a large bowl, mix the ground lamb and lamb fat until well mashed and smooth.

Add the ginger, garlic, and browned onion pastes along with some salt and the red chili powder. Set aside in the refrigerator for 2 hours.

Add the roasted gram dal, garam masala, awadhi masala, saffron water, and kewra water and mix well.

Make a hole in the center and place a small bowl of live charcoal with the clove powder in it. Cover the large bowl for 10 minutes to allow the mince to absorb the smoky flavor.

Mold the ground lamb into small patties. Heat a griddle over a medium heat, brush with a little ghee, and cook the patties on both sides until done.

Garnish with mint sprigs and serve with onion rings.

At Masala Bay, they place the galouti kebabs on small parathas slightly larger than the galoutis themselves. Chef Kumar calls them "ulta tawa parathas."

Bhatti Da Murgh

TANDOORI CHICKEN

200g natural yogurt, hung in muslin
    for 4 hours
50g bhatti masala (see page 154)
2 plump chickens, skinned and
    quartered into two breasts
    and two legs each
50g ginger paste (see page 155)
50g garlic paste (see page 155)
juice of 5 limes
100g ghee, for basting (see page 155)
salt to taste

serves 8

Shah Rukh Khan's famed love of tandoori chicken is turned into a delicacy in the hands of Executive Chef Jitendra Kumar of The Taj Land's End, Mumbai. An authentic version, this delectable Indian roast chicken has two unique aspects – the spicy coating and the smoky flavour of the tandoor. Of course few people in India have their own tandoor nowadays and so the flavour can be reproduced by other cooking methods – see below.

Mix the bhatti masala into the yogurt and leave overnight in the fridge.

Take the chicken pieces and coat them with the ginger and garlic pastes. Put them in a shallow dish and cover with lime juice. Set aside for 2 hours to marinate in the refrigerator.

Make several slashes into the flesh of each piece of chicken and coat each with some yogurt and masala mix. Spear a strong skewer through each chicken piece and cook in your tandoor for 10 minutes. Baste with ghee and return to the tandoor for a further 10 minutes.

These are equally good if you barbecue them: the best option is the open spit barbecue grill. It will provide a little of the smoky effect that tandoor cooking is all about. There is no need for skewers – place the chicken pieces on the grill and cook for about 25–30 minutes then turn and cook for the same time on the other side, taking care not to let them burn.

You can also use a conventional oven – preheat to 180°C/350°F/gas mark 4. Roast the chicken pieces on a tray for 30 minutes. Remove the tray and baste the chicken pieces with ghee, turning them over. Reduce the heat to 160°/325°F/gas mark 3 and cook for further 30 minutes.

Serve hot, with mint chutney, onion rings and slices of lime.

Kovalam Pomfret

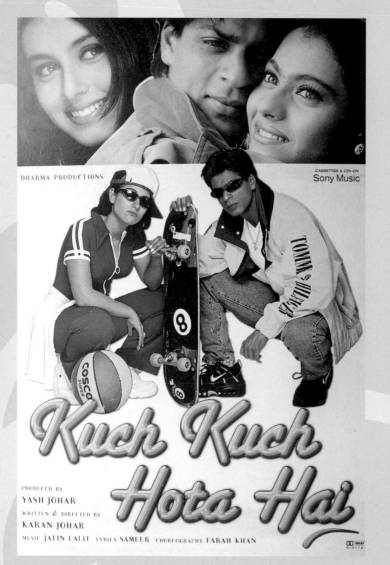

1½oz ginger-garlic paste (see page 155)
1½ tablespoons lemon juice
6 pomfret fillets (or other firm white fish)
5oz coconut, shredded
1oz yellow chili powder
2½oz chat masala (see page 154)

serves 6
1 cup split black lentils (urad dal)
¾ cup basmati rice
2 teaspoons red chili powder
1oz curry leaves, fried
3oz garlic, roughly chopped and fried to crisp light brown
salt to taste

This recipe makes a great appetizer. Lightly prepared without oil, it is crunchy on the outside with robust flavors.

Mix the ginger-garlic paste, a little salt, and half the lemon juice in a bowl. Coat the fillets with the mixture and set aside to marinate for 5 minutes.

Make a paste with the coconut, yellow chili powder, half the chat masala and the remaining lemon juice.

Grind the urad dal and rice into a powder and mix with the remaining chat masala, the red chili powder and the fried curry leaves.

Coat the fish with the coconut paste and then cover with the powder mix.

Dry-fry the fish in a tawa (griddle pan) or a non-stick skillet for 2 minutes, then turn over and cook for a further 1–2 minutes. Oil-free frying gives the fish a really delicious, crispy texture.

Garnish with the fried garlic and serve hot.

Langarwali Dal

3¾ cups split black lentils
  (urad dal)
4oz gram dal (channa dal)
salt to taste
1 teaspoon turmeric
3oz ghee (see page 155)
1oz piece of fresh ginger root, peeled
  and chopped
¾oz green chiles, chopped
½oz cumin seeds
1 medium tomato, chopped
1 tablespoon red chili powder
1 tablespoon ground coriander
a large handful of cilantro leaves

serves 6

Black lentils are a staple in the north of India and this dish takes its name from the free meal service (langar) offered in gurudwaras (Sikh temples), at which dal and rotis are a requisite. Cooked overnight with the simplest ingredients, it is delicious and fragrant. The husks of the lentils are removed before you buy them so that this dish is not black at all.

In a large pan put both dals, some salt, the turmeric, and about 3½–5 pints of water and cook, covered, over a low flame for 1 hour and 10 minutes until wellcooked. The water should have been absorbed. You can use a pressure cooker, in which case reduce the quantity of water by half and cook for 25 minutes after the cooker has reached pressure.

In a pan, heat the ghee and sauté the ginger, green chiles, and cumin seeds for 1–2 minutes. Add the tomato, red chili powder, and ground coriander and cook for a further 5 minutes.

Add this to the cooked dal and cook for a further 5 minutes. Serve hot, sprinkled with fresh cilantro leaves, and accompany with tandoori rotis, chapattis, or naan bread.

Amrita Arora has a vitality that is very appealing. Fondly called "Amu," Malaika Arora's younger sister is confident, clear-headed, and charming. Like most young girls growing up watching Bollywood films, she was addicted to the films of Madhuri Dixit and Sridevi. "They inspired me to be an actress, as much as my sister did." Amrita watched with admiration as her sister practiced for the incomparable "Chaiyya Chaiyya" song sequence in *Dil Se* (1998) with Shah Rukh Khan and this deepened her resolve to become a part of Bollywood.

Amrita started her career by winning the MTV VJ Hunt, and hosted shows like "MTV Houseful" and "Chill Out" for over two years. "I grew up watching this channel so it was amazing to have such a ball hosting shows, doing gigs and earning all that pocket money!" She was at the Natraj Studio filming an advertising campaign when she met Aamir Khan who predicted "You will definitely be an actress one day." Amrita does not think he remembers that, but for her they were the nicest words anyone could have said to her.

Amrita Arora

Her initial films did not do well but she was unfazed and continued to take on parts with zeal and determination. Her efforts were rewarded with a string of hit films. *Girlfriend* (2004), her most visible and controversial film, dealt with the theme of lesbianism. While the moral brigade and media tore the film to shreds, Amrita spoke up to defend it with commendable rationality and clarity. Her song sequence "Dilli Ki Sardi" in the film *Zameen* (2003) has become incredibly well known and provided an opportunity for her to work with directors like Mahesh Manjrekar—"He really pushes the boundaries of his actors"—and Vikram Bhatt—"You have to unlearn everything with him and then learn so much. He is from a different school of acting altogether."

Amrita loves London because it has an "electric vibe" and she often meanders around central London, relaxing in cafés and window-shopping. "I like the Edgware Road district with its Lebanese, Arabic, and Iranian communities and food. Another favorite is Chai in Primrose Hill, who do a wonderful variety of teas and desserts and even serve a masala tea from India." Amrita's boyfriend, Usman Afzal, is a cricketer with the English team. She loves to watch him play, accompanied by a basket of French fries with Mexican chili. She is also addicted to watching British sitcoms like *Nighty Night, Only Fools and Horses,* and *Footballers' Wives.*

Food is very much a part of Amrita's childhood memories. "We are lovers of fish. My mother is from Kerala so a lot of food cooked at home is part of Kerala cuisine." Kerala cuisine always evokes wonderful memories for Amrita, and she shared some of her favorites as well as some classics.

Avial

1 fresh coconut, shredded
6 whole green chiles
1 tablespoon cumin seeds, roasted
14oz sour yogurt (yogurt kept in
    cheesecloth in a warm place
    overnight)
9oz yam, peeled and cut into
    1½in cubes
9oz ash gourd (or pumpkin) peeled
    and cut into 1½in cubes
3 bananas, peeled and cut into
    1½in pieces
3 drumsticks, scaled and cut into
    2in pieces (optional)
2 potatoes, peeled and quartered
2 cups peas
¾ teaspoon turmeric
3½ tablespoons coconut oil or
    vegetable oil
6–8 curry leaves
salt to taste

serves 6

This dish is very popular in Kerala and, when made without the oil, it is healthy and light. The vegetables in it are specific to Kerala and can be replaced with carrots, beans, and other gourds. Drumsticks are a local vegetable but hard to find in the West, and can be omitted.

Make a paste with the shredded coconut, green chiles, and cumin seeds, adding a little water. Add this paste to the sour yogurt and set aside.

Cook the vegetables in ¾ cup of water in a heavy saucepan with some salt and the turmeric. When cooked, add the paste and remove from the heat. Add the coconut oil and curry leaves. Mix well.

Serve hot, with rice.

Note: coconut oil has a strong flavor that coastal Indians enjoy; one way to tone down the flavor is to heat the vegetable oil and fry the curry leaves in it before adding them to the dish.

Payasam

300g brown rice or short-grain rice
1 litre milk
500g jaggery or soft brown sugar
100g coconut, grated
150g ghee (see page 155)
1 tablespoon cardamom powder
75g cashew nuts
50g raisins

serves 6

Payasam is integral to Kerala's temple culture, a dessert that is considered to be the food of the Gods. It differs from kheer, the rice and milk pudding eaten across India, in that jaggery is used instead of sugar, giving it an earthy aroma and flavour. Jaggery is made from palm sugar and has a unique taste. If unavailable, use cane sugar jaggery or soft brown sugar.

Wash the rice thoroughly and soak it in cold water for 10 minutes. Drain it and put it into a large pan with the milk. Bring it to simmering point and cook for 30 minutes until the rice becomes very soft.

Crumble the jaggery and add it to the rice. Stir while cooking and allow the jaggery to dissolve. Then add the coconut and half the ghee. Stir and allow the mixture to boil until it has a thick consistency and the aroma of the jaggery fills the air. Stir in the cardamom powder and remove from the heat.

Heat the remaining ghee in a small pan and fry the cashew nuts until they brown slightly. Add the raisins and quickly remove from the heat.

Garnish the payasam with the nuts and raisins. Serve warm.

Sambhar

4oz red gram dal (arhar or toor dal)
½ teaspoon turmeric
2 whole green chiles
10 pearl onions, whole, or 3 large onions, halved
1 drumstick, chopped into 1½in pieces (a local vegetable that can be hard to find—optional)
2 medium potatoes, peeled and quartered
3 tomatoes, chopped
1 eggplant, halved lengthways and cut into 1½in wedges (optional)
2 tablespoons tamarind paste
2 tablespoons coconut oil
¼ teaspoon asafoetida
10 curry leaves
2 red chiles, split in half
1 tablespoon black mustard seeds
salt to taste

FOR THE SAMBHAR MASALA
3 tablespoons coriander seeds
1 tablespoon cumin seeds
4 dry chiles, stalks removed and seeded
3oz coconut, shredded
2 tablespoons gram dal (channa dal)
2 tablespoons fenugreek seeds

serves 6

This dal preparation is made throughout southern India and eaten in homes almost every day. At the heart of the dish is the sambhar masala. Though available as a proprietary masala, try to make this yourself as store-bought versions cannot match it for flavor. It can be stored in a dry, airtight jar for up to a year. It acts as both a thickening agent and a spice in this simple recipe.

Make the sambhar masala by dry-roasting all the ingredients in a small skillet until they are light brown and have released their aromas. Leave to cool then grind.

Put the red gram dal in a heavy saucepan and add 4 cups of water, the turmeric, and salt and bring to a boil. Reduce the heat to simmering point and add the green chiles, onions, drumstick, and potatoes. Cook for 20 minutes then stir in the tomatoes and eggplant and continue cooking for a further 20 minutes. Then add the sambhar masala and tamarind paste.

In a small skillet, heat the coconut oil and add the asafoetida, curry leaves, red chiles, and mustard seeds. Stir this oil mixture into the dal and simmer for 10 minutes.

Serve hot, with rice, idlis, vadas, or dosas.

CURD RICE

2½ cups basmati rice
1¾lbs plain yogurt
scant ½ cup milk, if needed
2 small cucumbers, peeled and
   shredded
salt to taste

FOR THE TEMPERING
2 tablespoons ghee (see page 155)
pinch of asafoetida
1 tablespoon black mustard seeds
1½in piece of fresh ginger root, peeled
   and cut into julienne strips
3 dried whole red chiles
10 curry leaves

FOR THE GARNISH
a handful of cilantro leaves,
   chopped

serves 6

On a hot summer day, there is nothing more cooling and tasty than a bowl of curd rice. The dish, born in southern India, is simple to prepare. Traditionally, it is eaten at the end of the meal to calm the stomach.

Wash and soak the rice in cold water for 10 minutes. Drain, then cook in an open saucepan in 2½ pints of salted water. When the grains swell, cover the pan. When cooked, drain and allow the rice to cool on an open tray.

Beat the yogurt to give it a smooth consistency. Add the cooled rice and let it soak in the yogurt for 30 minutes. If the consistency is too dry or thick, add the milk to smoothen it. Mix in the cucumber.

In a skillet, heat the ghee and add the asafoetida, mustard seeds, ginger, whole red chiles, and curry leaves. Once all are spluttering, pour the spices over the curd rice and garnish with cilantro.

Serve cool or at room temperature. Curd rice goes well with pickles and poppadoms.

Variations include adding fruit pieces and using pomegranate seeds as decoration.

Kalan

½ medium green banana, peeled and
   sliced into 1½in pieces (optional)
4oz yam, peeled and cut into
   1½in cubes
4 green chiles, slit in half lengthways
¼ tablespoon turmeric
1 tablespoon freshly ground
   black pepper
1 tablespoon ghee (see page 155)
4 cups buttermilk or 18oz plain
   low-fat yogurt
1 small coconut, shredded
½ tablespoon cumin seeds, roasted
   and ground
½ tablespoon fenugreek powder
salt to taste

FOR THE SEASONING
1 tablespoon coconut oil
1 teaspoon black mustard seeds
2 dried red chiles
10 curry leaves

This dish from Kerala is made in many different ways across the state. The common characteristic is the use of buttermilk or yogurt, but the vegetables and spice mix vary. It is eaten as an alternative to a dal dish along with meat or fish. Green bananas have green skins and are a harder version of ripe bananas; they taste bland and starchy and are widely grown in Kerala. They can be omitted if you cannot find them.

Bring ⅔ cup of water to a boil in a saucepan. Add the green banana, yam, green chiles, turmeric, some salt, and the pepper, cover and cook until the water is absorbed. Pour in the ghee and stir.

Add the buttermilk, return to a boil and cook for 10 minutes, then mix in the shredded coconut and cumin seeds. Boil for a further 5 minutes.

In a separate small skillet, heat the coconut oil and add the black mustard seeds and the dried chiles. Take the pan off the heat when the mustard seeds darken and splutter, about 2 minutes. Add to the cooked kalan.

Serve hot, with boiled rice.

One needs to take a deep breath to introduce this fine actress: with 140 films, five national awards, 6 international awards, a Padma Shri, and retrospectives of her films at the New York film festival, Smithsonian Institute in Washington DC, and Pompidou Center in Paris, the list of her achievements is impressive. She is an impeccable actress and a vocal and committed social activist. She is the chairperson of Nivara Hakk (Right to Shelter) and also works on women's health, education, and economic empowerment. "I was brought up to believe that art should be used as a medium for social change and some of my films and roles have helped me do that." Her films *Arth* (1982) and *Fire* (1996) have become cult films and many women have found the characters she played hugely inspirational.

Shabana Azmi

"The hardest thing I find as an actress, is to have this elastic body where I have to gain and shed weight all the time." She made *Mandi* (1983) and *Khandhar* (1984) back to back; in *Mandi* she was a big brothel madam, for which she put on 26 pounds (helped by three breakfasts a day) and soon after had to lean out to play an emaciated Jamini. "Invariably I get to play these lean, poverty stricken, chased by hunger women and to be them physically is tougher than emoting the most complex emotions or learning the longest lines."

Born to a poet father, the late Kaifi Azmi, and an actress mother, Shaukat Kaifi, Shabana recalls an untroubled childhood filled with people and huge amounts of Hyderabadi food. She believes her mother is the most outstanding cook and hostess when it comes to Hyderabadi cuisine. Shabana recalls the elaborate tea ceremony her mother used to host, with the bone china teapot, tea cosy, and scented flowers in white and yellow that would always accompany the tea tray.

Shabana is passionate about food but does not seem to have her mother's instincts. "If you ask me to even look after a dish for two minutes, I will manage to burn it to cinders... I cannot cook, but every time I eat a good dish, I will seek its recipe and origin with intense zeal!" Her collection of recipes is now a fat book full of little notes, restaurant menus as markers, and hundreds of recipes.

Having grown up in Mumbai, Shabana loves to eat street food—samosas, bhelpuri, and bhajias (spicy fried snacks) are her passion. And she loves to eat eggs in all their forms. For two years at the film institute she ate egg bhurji (spicy scrambled eggs) and pao every single day for lunch, and friends will always make her an egg curry when she visits! She loves regional foods from India, especially the Gujarati thali, but despairs of Punjabi food in restaurants. "Give me Awadhi, Kerala, Rajasthani food...*real* Indian food."

Baghare

AUBERGINES HYDERABADI STYLE

1kg aubergines
3 tablespoons pure ghee (see page 155)
5 curry leaves
2 whole red chillies
2 tablespoons cumin seeds, roasted
  and ground
5 garlic cloves, peeled
1 teaspoon red chilli powder
1 teaspoon sesame seeds
2 tablespoons freshly grated coconut
2 tablespoons ground coriander
1½ tablespoons peanuts, roasted
  and ground
2 tablespoons tamarind, deseeded, soaked
  and made into paste
salt to taste

serves 6

At Mughal banquets this dish was an accompaniment to the many meats and biryanis on offer.

Wash and cut the aubergines into quarters.

Heat the pure ghee in a pan and add the curry leaves, red chillies, cumin seeds and garlic. Cook for 1 minute, add the aubergines and stir.

Season with some salt and add the red chilli powder, sesame seeds, coconut, coriander powder and ground peanuts. Cook for about 10 minutes on a low heat until the aubergines are tender. Add the tamarind paste and stir it in for a few minutes.

Serve hot, with roti, dal and salad.

Qabooli

GRAM LENTIL BIRYANI

6 tablespoons pure ghee (see page 155)
6 large onions, finely sliced
2 tablespoons ginger-garlic paste (see page 155)
4 green chiles, chopped
1½ teaspoons red chili powder
1 teaspoon cumin seeds, coarsely ground
seeds of 14 green cardamoms, ground (discard the husks)
4 whole green cardamom pods
4 cinnamon sticks
20–25 whole black peppercorns
6 cloves
4oz plain yogurt
2 handfuls mint leaves, chopped
2 handfuls cilantro leaves, chopped
9oz gram dal, (channa dal) soaked for 30 minutes
2lbs basmati rice, soaked for 30 minutes
2 tablespoons salt

serves 6

This unusual dish is a great way for vegetarians to enjoy a biryani. "Superb! To die for" is how Shabana describes it, and she often eats it at festivals like Id. This is a dum-cooked dish. Dum is a style of cooking developed in the royal kitchens in which food would be cooked in a sealed pot over a low heat. The taste of the meat and spices is more intense when cooked this way.

In a large saucepan, heat the pure ghee and fry the onions until lightly browned. Remove 2 tablespoons of the onions and reserve as a garnish. Add the ginger-garlic paste, green chiles, cumin seeds, cardamom seeds, cardamom pods, cinnamon, peppercorns, and cloves to the pan. Stir-fry them for 3 minutes then pour in the yogurt and continue cooking for a further 2 minutes.

Add the mint, cilantro, and the soaked gram dal. As the aroma intensifies, add 3 cups water and reduce the heat. Cover and cook for 30 minutes.

Boil the rice separately in 2½ pints of salted water until firm and partially cooked but not soft. Drain any excess water.

Separate the rice and cooked dal into 3 separate portions each. In a fresh saucepan, place alternating layers of rice and dal. Cover the pan and seal the edges of the lid—take some dough (as made for rotis or bread—see page 155) and use a ½ inch thick rolled strip to close the pan and lid. (As the pan heats up the flour strip hardens and seals the edges, stopping the steam from escaping and encouraging the flavors to combine.)

Place a tawa or a thick, flattish skillet on low heat and once hot, place the sealed biryani pan on it for 10 minutes. Remove the pan from the heat until it is time to serve.

Break the dough seal just before serving.

Sheer Kurma

3½ pints milk
1¾–2 cups granulated sugar
seeds of 10 green cardamoms
   (discard the husks)
pinch of cardamom powder
3 tablespoons pure ghee (see
   page 155)
3 cups fine vermicelli
⅓ cup raisins
½ cup shelled almonds, soaked,
   skinned and halved
⅓ cup shelled pistachios
⅓ cup shelled chirongi nuts
1 teaspoon freshly shredded nutmeg
1 teaspoon mace
2 tablespoons saffron strands,
   soaked in ½ cup cold milk
3 tablespoons pandanus water
   (kewra or pandan water) (optional)

serves 8–10

Great after a Hyderabadi Biriyani (see page 41), this is a classic dessert. Chirongi nuts (or cudpanuts) grow in Hyderabad, Maharastra, and Gujerat and they are used to garnish desserts such as halwas and cakes; they can be bought in Indian stores.

In a large saucepan over high heat, boil the milk with the sugar, cardamom seeds, and powder until the milk is reduced by half.

In a separate saucepan, heat the ghee and fry the vermicelli until it turns a deep shade of brown, then add the raisins and all the nuts. Pour the reduced milk into this and add the nutmeg and mace. Boil for 3 minutes, then pour in the saffron milk and pandanus water.

Can be served hot or cold.

Hyderabadi Biryani

FOR THE LAMB

2lbs lamb taken from the leg and cut into bite-sized pieces
18oz plain yogurt
9oz pure ghee (see page 155)
6 large onions, finely sliced
2 tablespoons ginger-garlic paste (see page 154)
2 large handfuls of mint leaves, chopped
2 large handfuls of cilantro leaves, chopped
4 green chiles, chopped
1½ teaspoons red chili powder
1½ teaspoons cumin seeds, coarsely ground
seeds of 14 green cardamoms, ground (discard the husks)
4 whole green cardamoms
4 cinnamon sticks, about 4in long
20–25 whole black peppercorns
6 cloves
salt to taste

FOR THE RICE

2lbs rice, soaked for 20 minutes
1 teaspoon garam masala (see page 154)
1 teaspoon saffron strands, soaked in 3½ tablespoons milk for 2 hours
juice of 2 limes
salt to taste

serves 8

This is a celebrated recipe from the Azmi home. Shabana's mother, Shaukat, is an exemplary cook who has had many decades of experience making traditional Muslim dishes. Shabana is now trying to put them together to make a recipe book. This wonderfully rich recipe is from the work in progress. Cooking time is 3–4 hours.

Marinade the lamb pieces in the yogurt for 1 hour or more.

In a large skillet, heat the pure ghee and add the onions, frying until they start to brown. Reduce the heat as soon as the color begins to change. (The color changes rapidly on a high heat. To avoid the onions burning, stir continuously over a low heat.)

Remove the onions from the ghee with a slotted spoon and place them on paper towels or on a large tray. Spread the onions to keep them crisp.

Add the marinated lamb to the ghee. Stir-fry for 5 minutes and add two-thirds of the fried onions, some salt, and all the herbs and spices and cook for 1 hour on a low heat. When the lamb is tender, set the pan aside.

To cook the rice, bring 2½ pints of water to a boil and add salt and the garam masala. Tip in the soaked rice. Cover the pan, reduce the heat and let the rice cook until it is firm but not soft (partially cooked—the water should have been absorbed). Divide the rice and lamb into 3 equal portions each.

In a large saucepan, place alternating layers of lamb and rice, finishing with a layer of rice. Gently mash the saffron strands into the milk. Pour the lime juice and saffron milk over the layers. Cover the pan with a tightly fitting lid and place a heavy weight over it, or seal the sides with wheat flour dough (see page 38).

Place a tawa or a thick, flattish skillet on a low heat and once hot, place the sealed biryani pan on it for 15 minutes. Remove the pan from the heat until it is time to serve—5 minutes is sufficient resting time.

Open the sealed pan and garnish with the remaining fried onions. Serve hot, with salad and raita.

opposite page:
Amitabh and Jaya Bachchan have been a popular on-screen couple in many films. They recently came together in *Kabhi Khushi Kabhie Gham* (2001) as the Raichands, the couple for whom the tag line "It's all about loving your parents" was created.

Amitabh Bachchan, fondly referred to as "Big B," has achieved an incredible stature in India. Recently, when he needed to be operated on for an intestinal disorder, the huge media interest around the world was a tribute to the power he wields in his quiet, unassuming way. At sixty-three, his performances are finely etched and subtle and producers continue to furiously write scripts for him. He turned around the fortunes of an Indian television channel with the show *Kaun Banega Crorepati* (the Indian version of *Who Wants to Be a Millionaire*) and is quite simply the national icon of success.

The Bachchans

below: The Bachchans have always been a close-knit family—in keeping with the classic Indian tradition, Amitabh Bachchan's parents lived with them, as does his son Abhishek.

The soul of the Bachchan home is his wife, Jaya Bachchan. Born to a Bengali home, she grew up loving eggs: "I loved the Indian recipe for Russian salad, just because it had lots of boiled eggs!" She continues to relish Bengali cuisine, which she now makes in a lighter style, with less heavy masalas and oil. She describes herself as a food purist. She always attempts to give primacy to the original flavor of the main ingredient in her cooking, be it vegetable, meat, or fish, and she takes care to retain the texture, color, and freshness of the flavors.

When dining out, Nelson Wang's China Garden in Mumbai was a favorite family haunt, although it is more difficult for them to visit it now that it has moved to a more public place in a shopping mall. Jaya speaks fondly of the tasty kebabs at the Sun and Sand Hotel in Juhu, Mumbai. It is a place that she feels has retained its quality and reputation through the years.

The family loves Indian cuisine—when traveling the first thing Jaya will do is research the best places where they can find good local food. Amitabh is vegetarian while Jaya and their son, Abhishek, both enjoy fish and meat. "It's tough to be vegetarian when you leave India and though Amitabh will sample a pasta now and then what he really craves and what comforts him more than anything else, is a simple vegetable dal and chapatti." So, during a recent stay in New York, he found a Gujarati cook to make him fresh home cooked food every day. Sunday lunches at their home in Juhu are invariably South Indian feasts, and dosas and idlies are family favorites.

above: Amitabh and Abhishek Bachchan have come together in a few films like *Bunty Aur Babli* (2005), *Sarkar* (2005), and most recently *Kabhi Alvida Na Kehna* (2006), the new Karan Johar film.

page 46: Abhishek Bachchan as an ubercool conman in Rohan Sippy's *Bluffmaster.* (2006). Interestingly, Abhishek and Rohan's fathers worked together in the 1970s and '80s as actor and director to make films like *Sholay* (1975) and *Shakti* (1982).

pages 48–49: The senior Raichand (Amitabh Bachchan, center) flanked by his two sons Rohan (Hrithik Roshan) and Rahul (Shah Rukh Khan) in the 2001 hit film *Kabhi Khushi Kabhie Gham.* Here they can be seen dancing to the well-known "Shaava Shaava

The younger Bachchan, Abhishek, is an exciting actor who is lucky enough to combine the finest skills from each of his parents. His performances have his mother's spontaneity and impish charm, and his father's intense presence and gravity. His performances in *Yuva* (2004) and *Bunty aur Babli* (2005) are evidence of his wide-ranging and diverse skills as an actor. He also has a splendid sense of humor which has made him very popular, especially with younger audiences.

At home with his family, Abhishek loves to tuck into potato cutlets (aaloo tikki), banana chips, and spicy savories (chiwda). He also has a penchant for fresh cottage cheese in butter masala (paneer makhani) and spicy tandoori chicken in butter masala.

There is graciousness to the premier star family of Bollywood, who represent the finest of cultural traditions. They are respected throughout the Bollywood film industry and are much loved by their multitudes of fans.

Hara Channa Masala

MUNG BEANS AND SCALLIONS

2 tablespoons vegetable oil
4 scallions (use the bulb and 3in green stem), sliced
18oz fresh mung beans, shelled
1 tablespoon garam masala, freshly ground if possible (see page 154)
salt to taste

serves 6

This delightful dish is a family favorite and utterly simple to prepare. Mung beans are grown in the winter in northern India and are cooked in the pod on an open fire. The pods open with a splutter and the hot mung bean, or green gram, is eaten plain or spiced with lemon juice. Simple and delicious!

In a pan, heat the oil and sauté the scallions for 2–3 minutes, then add the mung beans. Cover and cook on a low heat for about 10 minutes until they squash easily between your fingers. Season with some salt.

Sprinkle with garam masala and serve hot, with rotis and dal.

Aachari Aaloo

POTATOES IN PICKLE MASALA

2 tablespoons vegetable oil
2 onions, finely chopped
3 tomatoes, skinned and chopped
1 teaspoon turmeric
8 large potatoes, peeled and quartered
2 tablespoons mango pickle masala
a handful of cilantro, chopped
salt to taste

serves 6

Mango pickle is the most commonly used pickle in India; here only the juices and not the pieces of mango are used—this is called mango pickle masala.

Heat the oil in a large skillet. Fry the onions over a high heat, stirring them continuously until they turn medium brown. Add the tomatoes and keep stirring until the mixture turns into a smooth paste.

Season with some salt and the turmeric and after 1 minute add the potatoes and 3½ tablespoons of water. Cover the pan and cook the potatoes for about 20 minutes on a low heat. The water will have evaporated.

When the potatoes are tender, add the mango pickle masala (not the mango pieces) and stir in. Garnish with chopped cilantro and serve hot, with rotis, dal, and raita.

Aaloo Tikki aur Pudine ki Chutney

POTATO CUTLETS WITH MINT CHUTNEY

FOR THE MINT CHUTNEY
9oz mint leaves
1 large onion, finely chopped
2 large whole green chiles
juice of 3 lemons
½ teaspoon rock salt
½ teaspoon black pepper

FOR THE CUTLETS
3½lbs potatoes, boiled, peeled, cooled, and mashed
2 tablespoons cumin seeds, roasted and ground
1 tablespoon freshly ground black pepper
6 teaspoons vegetable oil
salt to taste

serves 6

This is Abhishek Bachchan's favorite dish, and it's very popular with the whole family. Across India, there are variations on the stuffings, from mashed peas to spice blends, but the Bachchans prefer it simple and don't stuff theirs. Mint chutney is always prepared from the fresh herb and not kept overnight, as the flavor deteriorates quickly.

To make the mint chutney, whizz the ingredients in a blender and set aside.

Combine the mashed potatoes with the ground cumin seeds, black pepper and salt to taste. Shape the mixture into 12 cutlets.

Heat a little oil in a skillet on a medium heat. Place the potato cutlets gently into the pan, cook for 1 minute then increase the heat. Turn them over and continue to cook. Perfect cutlets are crisp on both sides and golden brown in color.

Place on paper towels to drain the oil and serve piping hot with the chutney.

SHRIMP IN GREEN VEGETABLES

2 tablespoons vegetable oil
1 tablespoon Bengali panch phoren
   (a mixture of equal parts whole cumin
   seeds, fenugreek seeds, mustard seeds,
   black onion seeds, and fennel seeds)
18oz raw tiger shrimp, de-veined
18oz baby spinach, roughly chopped
leaves of 3 radishes, roughly chopped
   (optional)
1 small white cabbage, roughly chopped
a pinch of sugar
salt to taste

serves 6

Jaya Bachchan has adapted this from a more elaborate Bengali dish to make it lighter and keep the taste of both shrimp and vegetables intact.

Heat the oil in a saucepan and fry the Bengali panch phoren until it darkens slightly. Add the shrimp and keep turning them over until they turn a light shade of pink.

Add the spinach, radish leaves, and cabbage, cover the pan and steam-cook for 10 minutes. Season with some salt and sugar and mix gently. Allow to cook until water from the vegetables reduces; they should be just crunchy.

Serve hot, with rice and dal.

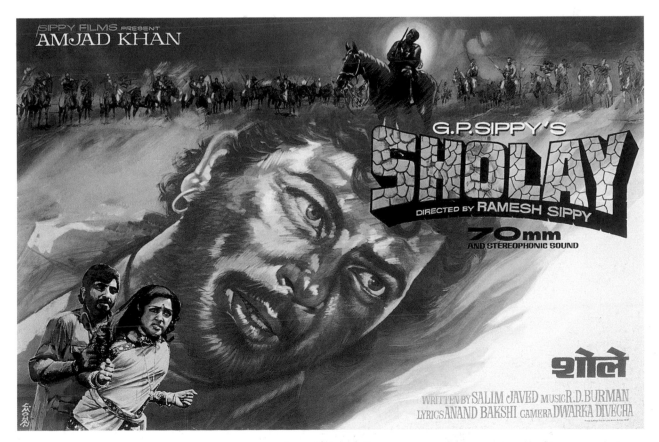

Known for his chiseled features and intense gaze, Rahul Bose has shaped an intelligent and interesting career in Bollywood. His recent work in *Mr & Mrs Iyer* (2002), *Mumbai Matinée* (2003), and *Kaalpurush* (2005) exhibits a wonderful sense of control and his ability to give credibility to the characters he plays. He started acting on stage, moving to cinema with a part in the cult film *English, August* (1994) and has never looked back. He has recently also tried his hand at directing and is extremely proud of his directorial debut, a small independent film, *Everybody Says I am Fine* (2002).

And he loves his food.

He speaks of food with an emotional energy and total sense of recall. "As a child I used to be fascinated by the brightly lit sweet shops of Kolkata. At puja time the sweets would be in shapes of lotuses, aeroplanes, spaceships. Those sandesh, colorful rosgullas, chum-chums. Unforgettable. I may use it in a film someday."

Rahul Bose

Three Ks rule Rahul's palate—Kolkata, Kasauli, and Kolhapur—each with a different culinary character. He finds the spicy foods of Kolhapur masculine and full-bodied, while he delights over the subtle grace of Bengali cooking. Kasauli in summer meant Punjabi meals with the neighbors: parathas, lassi, and watermelons. Yet the best cooking came from his father—Rupen Bose loves to cook. For his daughter's wedding reception, he cooked for 125 people. "It took him three days, but what a meal!"

"My most enduring food memories are not in the eating of it but in the shopping for it. In Bengal, it is the man who does the shopping. On Sundays, my father would take me along to the bazaars. Before buying, we would sample the peas and check the baingan (eggplant) skin for firmness and plumpness, the ends of bhindis (okra) and beans would be cracked to check for freshness. I had to hold my father's index finger through this whole journey and to me that finger felt stronger than a tree trunk."

He reminisces about a wonderful meal in Gwalior: on a freezing frosty January morning, at about 3 a.m., the only place open was a tiny dhabha. They sat on gunny-covered charpoys and were served whatever was available—thin mutton curry, fresh peas and tomatoes, and tandoori roti. "The peas were sweet and popped in my mouth. It was their freshness. As any chef in the world will vouch for, the best food is when the natural and fresh flavors are brought out."

Rahul is a fan of Hindustani classical music. He remembers concerts that he used to attend as a young child, when all the maestros were Turkish children. It was during these musical soirees that he developed another food fetish: the paan (a betel leaf usually stuffed with nuts and condiments). Over thirty years he has evolved the perfect one for himself—Kolkata sweet leaf with kathaa, less chuna than usual, one cardamom, one clove, a little bit of laxmi bahar (a sweet paste), and peppermint. Delicious!

Widely traveled, Rahul has sampled cuisines from all over India. He rates Ananda Solomon as his favorite chef and the Sonar Goan at the Taj Bengal as the best Indian restaurant. Rahul takes a real interest in the food he eats. He can give you historic accounts of the development of Bengali cuisine and describe which elements of Awadhi and colonial British influences were absorbed to create the modern dishes eaten today. Rahul does not cook much himself, but his alertness and attention to food and its history is certainly impressive.

JHAAMUU SUGHAND
PRESENTS

PJ. SUGHAND PRODUCTIONS '

Memories in the Mist...

A FILM BY BUDDHADEB DASGUPTA

MITHUN CHAKRABORTHY   RAHUL BOSE   SAMEERA REDDY   SUDIPTA CHAKRABORTHY   LABONY SARKAR
CAMERAMAN SUDIP CHATTERJEE   SOUND ANUP MUKHOPADHYAY   ART DIRECTOR SAMIR CHANDA   EDITOR SANJIB DUTTA   ONLINE PRODUCER DULAL K. RAY
ASSOC. DIRECTORS ARUN GUHA THAKURTA   SOHINI DASGUPTA   MUSIC BISWADEB DASGUPTA   EXECUTIVE PRODUCER SANJAAY ROUTRAY
PRODUCER JUGAAL SUGHAND   STORY, SCRIPT & DIRECTION BUDDHADEB DASGUPTA

opposite page: Rahul Bose has been the face of experimental cinema in recent years—his directorial debut, *Everybody Says I Am Fine* (2002) showed modern Mumbai's people and their chaotic interiors.

above: Budhadhadeb Dasgupta's film *Kaalpurush* has Rahul Bose playing a man married to an ambitious wife. It explores the dilemmas of success and father-son relationships.

Shaami Kebabs

KABOB CUTLETS

3½lbs ground lamb

9oz split gram dal (channa dal),
   soaked for 20 minutes

1½ teaspoons red chili powder

3 tablespoons ginger-garlic paste (see
   page 155)

1 teaspoon garam masala
   (see page 154)

2 teaspoons salt

3 medium onions, finely chopped

5 green chiles, finely diced

a large handful of cilantro, chopped

a large handful of mint leaves, chopped

2–3 tablespoons vegetable oil

Serves 6

Among Rahul's close set of friends is Faisal, whose mother, Mrs Naseem Siddiqui, makes the best shaami kabobs and shared this recipe. In the traditional method of cooking, the mutton or lamb would be hand-ground rather than ground in a blender. The traditional accompaniment is kachumber, a relish of finely chopped onions, cucumbers, tomatoes, and red chiles in lemon juice and salt.

Put the lamb in a large saucepan and add the dal, chili powder, ginger-garlic paste, and garam masala. Mix in a generous sprinkling of salt and add ¾ cup of water. Bring to a boil, discard any froth on the surface, then cover the pan and simmer for 45 minutes on low heat. Allow the water to evaporate, then remove from the heat and leave the mix to cool. Whizz in a blender for 2 minutes.

Tip the meat mixture into a bowl and mix in the onions, chiles, cilantro, and mint. Shape into 12 kabob cutlets.

In a non-stick skillet, using minimal oil, fry the kabobs until both sides are crisp and golden brown.

Serve hot, with mint chutney and kachumber. Shaami kabobs also go well with sweet mango or lemon chutney.

THE GREAT BENGALI TOMATO CHUTNEY

2lbs tomatoes
4oz jaggery (cane or palm
   sugar—use soft brown
   sugar as a substitute)
10 dates, pitted
10 dried apricots, pitted
⅓ cup golden raisins
2 tablespoons mustard oil
1 tablespoon black or white
   mustard seeds
salt to taste

This is a great finger-licking chutney and Rahul's father, Rupen Bose considers it to be essential to a good Bengali meal. It will last for a few days if refrigerated.

First, skin the tomatoes: make a cross with a sharp knife on the base and drop them into a bowl of boiling water. Remove after 1 minute and place under cold running water. Take off the skins by pulling from the slit of the cross. Cut each tomato into four.

Heat a pan and add the quartered tomatoes, jaggery, dates, apricots, and raisins. Sprinkle with a little salt and cook on a low heat for 10 minutes using a ladle to smoothen the tomatoes and the dried fruits. The jaggery will dissolve into the mix.

In a small skillet, heat the mustard oil to smoking point and add the mustard seeds. Remove when the mustard seeds start popping, about 1 minute, and add to the chutney.

Serve cool. A tangy, fruity accompaniment to any Indian meal, particularly Bengali.

Mutton Chop Masala

LAMB CHOP MASALA

2 tablespoons coriander seeds
1 teaspoon cumin seeds
3½lbs lamb ribs, rinsed
 and dried
3 tablespoons salt
2 tablespoons turmeric
1 tablespoon red chili powder
1 small green papaya, peeled and
 pulped to a paste
3 tablespoons vegetable oil
2oz lamb fat (get the butcher to give
 you this)
juice of 2 lemons
¼oz saffron strands, soaked in
 1½ tablespoons water for 10 minutes

serves 6

Rahul's father is a keen cook. When he gives his recipes, there is an assured manner—for this dish he painstakingly explained that goat is preferable to lamb or mutton because the flesh is a deeper red when raw, which provides a more intense flavor. He advised getting one rib bone removed by the butcher for more meat and partly smashing the other for more flavor. This dish was originally created by the Masjid community of Kolkata. You can of course use lamb.

Roast the coriander seeds and cumin seeds until they turn a darker shade. Hand-grind them into a coarse powder or whizz in a grinder for 5 seconds; the seeds should retain some body.

Mix this powder with the salt, tumeric, red chili powder, and green papaya paste and use to coat the ribs. Leave to marinate for 1 hour 30 minutes, turning the ribs over a couple of times.

In a large shallow skillet, heat the oil with lamb fat and when the fat has melted add in the ribs one at a time. As they fry, tilt the pan to one side to add the new pieces in the oil. When the ribs are crisp, remove them and pour 1 cup of water into the oil left in the pan and let it boil for a few minutes. Put the ribs back in the pan, cover and simmer for 30 minutes or until the meat is soft. The water will evaporate away. Add the lemon juice and saffron water and stir briefly.

Serve hot, with rotis or bread.

Baingan Ka Bharta

GRILLED EGGPLANT MASALA

3 large eggplants

FOR THE MASALA
5 tablespoons vegetable oil
4 large onions, chopped
6 garlic cloves, chopped
1½in piece of fresh
   ginger root, peeled and
   chopped
3 teaspoons ground coriander
1 teaspoon red chili powder
⅓ cup light cream
a bunch of cilantro, chopped
salt to taste

serves 6

Rahul loves this vegetable dish and his favorite version is made by his friend's mother, Tutu Thukral, whose recipe is below. The beauty of this dish is the smoky flavor and the best versions are those that are roasted in the right way. In the old days cooks would throw the eggplant into the tandoor and pick them out after 10 minutes. The roadside dhabas of the north still use this method.

Roast the eggplant over a gas flame, turning them until the skin crackles and breaks. Allow them to cool, then peel off the skins. Run under tap water to remove any remaining blackened skin. Mash the eggplant and set aside.

In a large skillet, heat the oil and sauté the onions until light brown. Add the garlic and ginger and continue to cook for a few more minutes. Add the ground coriander and chili powder. Cook for a further 3–4 minutes until the oil begins to separate out of the mix, then stir in the cream. After 1 minute add the mashed eggplant. Season with salt, mix well and cook for a further 3–4 minutes. Garnish with chopped cilantro.

Another version uses tomatoes, green chiles and sweet garden peas. Add them after the onions have browned.

Dal

LENTILS

¾ cup lentils
2 tablespoons pure ghee
   (see page 155)
1 small onion, chopped
4 garlic cloves, finely chopped
salt to taste

serves 6

Rahul is a big fan of dals in all their various forms—they are his comfort food. This recipe from his father is simple and light. Wash the lentils thoroughly in running water before cooking.

Bring 2 cups water to a boil, add some salt and the tumeric, and tip in the rinsed lentils. Return to the boil, then reduce the heat and simmer for 20 minutes, or until the dal has swelled and the water has evaporated.

In a small skillet, heat the pure ghee and add the chopped onion and garlic. Fry till light brown, then add to the lentils. Dal can be accompanied by rice or chapattis and vegetables.

Shosher Machch

FISH IN MUSTARD SAUCE

¾oz black mustard seeds, soaked in a
    little water overnight and drained
1 large fresh water carp or rainbow
    trout (about 4½lbs when whole)
1 teaspoon turmeric
1 tablespoon salt
5 tablespoons mustard oil
3 large onions, roughly chopped
2 green chiles, seeded
    and quartered
juice of 2in piece of fresh ginger root
3 tablespoons plain yogurt
a handful of cilantro leaves

serves 6

The artfully laid out selection of fish was a highlight of Rahul's childhood shopping trips with his father, Rupen. Rupen's recipe for Shosher Machch is a lighter version of the classic Bengali dish.

Grind the soaked mustard seeds coarsely.

Descale and fillet the fish (a fish merchant can do this for you). Cut it into large pieces with the skin on. (Both head and tail are traditionally cooked in this dish, but are optional.)

In a large dish mix the tumeric, salt, and half the mustard oil, then stir in the fish pieces and leave to marinate for 5–10 minutes.

Heat the remaining mustard oil in a large skillet and sauté the onions until they turn light brown. Add the fish pieces one at a time and turn them as they firm up and lose their translucency. Add the ground mustard seeds, green chiles, ginger juice, and yogurt. Stir gently to coat the fish evenly and continue to cook for a further 3 minutes; avoid moving the fish around the pan as the flesh tends to break up. (Rupen Bose avoids this problem by finishing the cooking in the microwave.)

Garnish with cilantro leaves and serve hot, with steamed rice.

Like an eagle, Nandita Das flies at an angle, one wing tipped earthward and the other skyward. Her roots are in Delhi, where she studied for a Masters degree in social work. A chance role in *Fire* (1996)—a provocative film on sexuality—catapulted her into a career as an actress, but she remains committed to her social work. Indeed, she often chooses film roles that mirror the tough realities she has dealt with first-hand. In *Bhawander* (2001), a film based on a true story, she played the victim of a gang rape fighting for justice in rural Rajasthan.

Her career ranges from international films to Indian films in many different languages—Nandita has few barriers. She has also directed short films on social concerns and is working on the script of her first feature film. She is a modern woman, an Indian at heart who is able to balance her social concerns with her love of films.

Nandita Das

Her father, the painter Jatin Das, loves to experience new and exciting culinary adventures. Nandita remembers his cooking as a flamboyant affair. There would always be an extensive guest list, elaborate cooking, and eye-catching presentation awash with color and design.

Nandita's strongest memories of food come from Baripada in Orissa, an eastern state in India and cultural sister to Bengal. She spent her summer vacations there, at the family home near the Jagannath Temple. Even the bhog (blessed food) from the temple tasted amazing, be it khichidi, dal, or sweets. She loves Oriya food for its subtle and singular tastes. There is far less use of spices in comparison to other Indian cuisines, and the tendency is to allow the flavor of the main ingredient to shine through. "Food is a combination of taste, smell, sight, and touch. For me, the memory of alphonso mangoes ripening in various corners of the house in different stages of color is unforgettable."

When it comes to eating out in Delhi, Nandita loves the melt-in-the-mouth kakori kabobs at Aap Ki Khatir and the south Indian food at Sagar in Defence Colony. She cooks occasionally, usually an upma or dalia with vegetables. "I think we have stopped listening to our instincts—we are being told all the time about some new theory so that we no longer listen to what our body wants to eat." When she returns from filming she looks forward to home-cooked food with its light, simple flavors and fresh ingredients.

opposite page: Nandita Das on location at Amravati for the film *Maati Maaye* (2006) directed by Chitra Palekar and based on the belief in witchcraft in rural Maharashtra.

Nandita believes that one of the best ways to unify the extremely diverse nation of India is by introducing different regional foods to people across the whole country. She feels very strongly that food can be used as a medium of cultural empathy, a way to break boundaries and create harmony between divided peoples and cultures.

Bhaddi Chura

DAL DUMPLINGS

FOR THE BHADDI
500g black lentils, skinned and split
    (urad dal dhuli)
2 tablespoons roughly ground
    black pepper
salt to taste

FOR THE CHURA
400g bhaddi
2 onions, ground to a paste
6 garlic cloves, ground to a paste
4 green chillies, ground to a paste
6 tablespoons mustard oil
salt to taste

serves 6

This dish comes from Orissa, an eastern state bordering Bengal. Variations of bhaddi, an urad dal paste dried in the sun, are used all over India. The Oriya and Bengali bhaddi is not as spicy as some. The lentils are white as the husks are removed. A stone mortar and pestle called a silbatta is used in Oriya and Bengali homes for spice-grinding.

Soak the lentils overnight in enough water to cover them by 3cm.

Blend the lentils with their soaking water into a really thick, smooth paste then stir in some salt and the pepper. On a well-greased tray, spoon out large portions of the lentils. Let them dry out in the sun for two days or place them in a low-heat oven (140°C/275°F/gas mark 1) for 2 hours. The portions will dry out and harden – these are called bhaddis.

Heat some oil in a frying pan and shallow fry the bhaddis in oil till they turn brownish. Once cool, break them using your fingers into a ground mixture (chura). Add the onion, garlic, green chilli paste, some salt and the mustard oil. They are a perfect accompaniment to Pokhaalo (see page 64).

Aaloo Poshto

POTATOES IN POPPY SEEDS

500g potatoes, peeled and diced
50g poppy seeds, soaked in water
    and drained
4 tablespoons mustard oil
3 large onions, finely chopped
2 teaspoons black onion seeds
    (kalonji)
salt to taste

Nandita recalls her aunt, Sarojini Patnaik, as a wonderful cook with an instinctive knack for making perfect dishes and serving them with love. This is her recipe.

Keep the prepared potatoes immersed in water until ready to cook as they tend to darken when exposed to air.

Grind the poppy seeds to a coarse paste.

Heat the mustard oil in a pan and sauté the onions until they turn light brown, then add the black onion seeds. Drain the potatoes and tip them in, along with the poppy seed paste and some salt. Cover and cook over a low heat until the potatoes are tender.

Serve hot, with rice.

Pokhaalo

FERMENTED RICE

1½ cups basmati rice
2 whole red chiles
2in piece of fresh ginger root,
   peeled and shredded
1 tablespoon ground
   cumin seeds
salt to taste

serves 6

This is simple traditional fare in Oriya homes. Nandita remembers this dish with great affection—it takes her back to many hot summer days in Baripada, where all her cousins would spend their summer holidays together. The recipe was shared by her cousin, Uttara Patnaik.

Cook the rice a day before making the pokhaalo. Wash the rice thoroughly and place it in about 3 cups of water (the water-to-rice ratio varies for each type of basmati rice, so experiment and you will get to know your rice). Bring to a boil, reduce the heat and simmer for about 15 minutes. When cooked, the rice grains will be long and soft.

Put the boiled rice in an unglazed clay pot and add water so it covers the rice by about 1¾in. Cover and leave overnight in a warm place to ferment.

Roast the red chiles by holding them by the stem over a flame for 1 minute. Leave to cool then crush them and add them to the rice and water. Mix in the shredded ginger, and ground cumin seeds.

Serve at room temperature. Pokhaalo is delicious with Bhaddi Chura (see page 62).

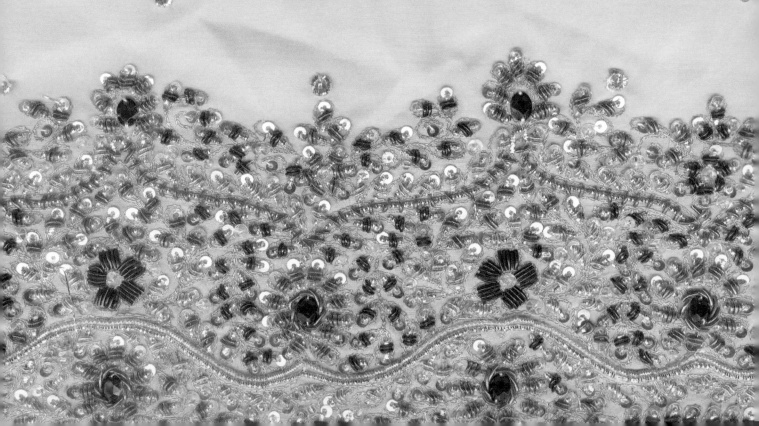

Dahi Baingan

EGGPLANT IN YOGURT

3 large eggplants
2 teaspoons salt
1 teaspoon turmeric
8 tablespoons mustard oil
9 garlic cloves, sliced
2 cups plain yogurt
1 tablespoon sugar
½ tablespoon asafoetida
6 curry leaves
1 tablespoon black mustard seeds
3 whole dried red chiles

serves 6

This is a Nandita Das special. She makes it for everybody because it is a real beat-the-heat dish and perfect for Delhi's hot months. It is also prepared very quickly, so is great for unexpected guests.

Cut the eggplant into ½–1in wide slices. Sprinkle them with half the salt and the turmeric.

Heat about 6 tablespoons of the mustard oil in a large skillet. Fry the sliced eggplant until they are brown and crisp on both sides. Halfway through the frying add the garlic. When done, place the eggplant and garlic on a serving dish.

Whip the yogurt until it's smooth. Add the remaining salt and the sugar and mix well. Pour this mixture over the cooked eggplant slices.

Heat the remaining mustard oil. Just as it begins to smoke add the asafoetida, curry leaves, mustard seeds, and chiles. Cook for 2 minutes, and then pour the mixture over the yogurt.

Leave to cool to room temperature, then refrigerate for 30 minutes.

Serve cold with rotis or rice, accompanied by dal, salad, and pickle.

With four generations of actors, producers, and directors, the Kapoor family certainly seems to have film in the blood. And their dining extravaganzas are as elaborate as the movies they make. The family comes from Peshawar in Pakistan, famed for the north-west frontier food whose deep influence lives on in the Kapoor's kitchen even today. Neetu Kapoor, Rishi Kapoor's wife, recalls her amazement at the breakfast table as a young bride. "There would be so much food: every kind of meat, eggs, paya soup, kheema…it was a revelation that so many things could be made." Amid the tables groaning with food spreads would be Raj Kapoor, eating his akuri and pao with simple pleasure.

The Kapoors

Prithviraj Kapoor, the patriarch, had a Herculean appetite and stories of his food feasts have become a part of Bollywood film lore. He was a large man with a deep voice, and his weight added to his grandeur. His obsessive love of food was passed on to all his sons (Raj, Shammi, and Shashi) and though they were handsome men in their youth they all battled with excess weight through middle age.

Raj Kapoor, the showman and creator of a distinct brand of "common man" cinema, was a great cook of biryanis and curries. Yet his personal tastes veered towards simple food: idlis, dosas, eggs, sandwiches. He continued to run a busy kitchen for his extended family and the constant flow of people visiting him. His lavish parties at Devnar Cottage are still remembered for the excellent feasts served. During weddings and festivals he and his wife were hosts beyond compare, with cuisines from all parts of the globe laid out in resplendence for their guests.

Raj's son, the actor Rishi Kapoor, was quick to fame after the success of his first film, *Bobby*, in 1973. His cherubic looks catapulted him to idol status and through three decades he has remained a prolific actor. In the late 1990s he began to take on smaller roles, though his youthful persona and great talent can still command a successful film. In the 80s he married his co-star of many hit films, Neetu Singh, a wonderfully svelte woman even after twenty-five years of Kapoor living. As Rishi acknowledges, "we have been great eaters—right from the days of my grandfather. It's a very involved relationship. We are the kind of people who live to eat—especially when there is good company. Neetu is extremely conscious of calories and cholesterol but the Kapoors are lovers of Peshawari non-vegetarian food. I am a beef-eating Hindu."

Neetu recalls that their courtship days were full of new food experiences as Rishi was quite a gourmet. During their travels, they would sample all sorts of fine foods and their favorites were Peter Luger's steaks in New York and hot pâté in morel sauce, first tasted in Gstaad, Switzerland.

Rishi loves Chinese food and has many memories of family outings in Mumbai to Nanking (once a respected restaurant, now closed down) and the restaurants of the Ling family. He will go to great lengths to find authentic Chinese food and learnt to use chopsticks early in life, so that he could enjoy the food as it was meant to be savored. "I was introduced to Punjabi food much later in life, when I joined films—things like tandoori chicken or chicken tikka. Home food was distinctly Peshawari. And let me tell you a secret, I hate hot food. Sometimes I also have mood swings and completely go off food, and prefer to just have a khichdi (non spicy dal and rice gruel)."

Another cuisine he loves is that of Kashmir. He speaks longingly of the wazawan (a Kashmiri food feast) tasted when he used to shoot films there, before the insurgency days. The wazawan menu extends to thirty-six courses, that are predominantly made up of meat. "Their spices are so natural and the flavor of the spinach is unique." A lot of the vegetables in Kashmir are grown on the floating gardens of the Dal Lake, that gives them a very distinct flavor that cannot be found anywhere else.

Rishi Kapoor has clearly taken after his father and his palate is refined. He cannot appreciate fast food and avoids it as much as possible. He likes his dishes full of flavor and spice. Although his father and uncles were good cooks he never took the time to learn the art himself. So now he prefers to eat good food rather than to cook it!

Kareena Kapoor, granddaughter of Raj Kapoor and the youngest film star from the great lineage of the Kapoor clan, voiced her intent to be an actress long before her older sister Karisma faced the camera for the first time. She grew up loving the old-style movies of Nargis, Madhubala, and Meena Kumari and the charm of classic 1950s cinema. She was confident one day she would be able to emulate her heroines and be a successful Bollywood actress.

Kareena Kapoor

Kareena's first film, *Refugee* (2000), created a lot of buzz and excitement as it also launched the career of Abhishek Bachchan. While the film was only a moderate success, both Kareena and Abhiskek got great reviews for their performances. Kareena, in particular, used her natural beauty to great advantage. Her minimal make-up was a refreshing look for Bollywood and her confidence astounding. She often mentioned that she always had a strong premonition that she would be an actress and was aware of the talent that lay within her. Many believed that her performance in *Refugee* was equal to that of a veteran actress.

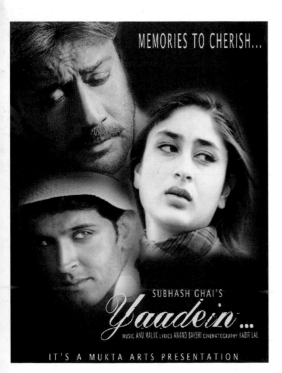

Kareena's next film, *Mujhe Kuch Kehna Hai* (2001), was a box-office hit and gave her early commercial success. She then went on to star in Santosh Sivan's *Asoka* (2001) with Shah Rukh Khan where she had an amazing ethereal look as the jungle warrior girl—her ethnic tattoos became very fashionable. Her talent and reputation was cemented and the role brought her the first of many Best Actress awards. She played a character that completely captured people's imaginations and established Kareena's strong connection with audiences. She began to represent the cool and individual attitude of today's modern youth. Young brands sought her out for advertising campaigns and she remains a favorite with the media.

Her acting continues to enthral. She made a foray into realistic cinema with *Chameli* (2003), playing the difficult role of a street-smart tough prostitute with grit. Her recent work with the director Vishal Bharadwaj will be interesting to watch—she has just finished *Omkara*, an adaptation of Shakespeare's *Othello,* and will also play the lead in his next film, *Mr Mehta & Mrs Singh*. She continues to go from strength to strength and at only twenty-six, Kareena clearly has a long and successful career ahead of her.

Chicken Haleem

½ cup yellow lentils (toor dal)
4oz split mung beans (moong dal)
4oz split gram dal (channa dal)
½ cup split red lentils (masoor dal)
½ cup black lentils (urad dal)
18oz chicken, boneless, diced
2 tablespoons ginger-garlic paste (see page 155)
3 green cardamoms
1 teaspoon turmeric
2 lemons
salt to taste

FOR THE TEMPERING
4oz pure ghee (see page 155)
4 onions, finely chopped
3 large tomatoes, skinned and chopped
2 tablespoons garlic paste (see page 155)
1½in piece of fresh ginger root, peeled and sliced
1 cinnamon stick
6 black peppercorns
2 black cardamoms
3 bay leaves
4 cloves
2 tablespoons coriander seeds
1 teaspoon turmeric
3 green or red chiles
pinch of ground coriander

FOR THE GARNISH
10 mint leaves
2 onions, sliced and fried until deep brown
1–2 red chiles, chopped
2 lemons, cut into wedges

serves 6

This dish comes from the aristocratic Hyderabadi cuisine.

Put the dals into a large saucepan with the chicken, ginger-garlic paste, green cardamoms, turmeric, and some salt, and cover with 3½ pints of water. Bring to a boil, then cover, reduce the heat and simmer for 1–1½ hours until the dals and the chicken are cooked. Leave to cool then mash all the ingredients together to a thick porridge-like consistency. Set aside.

For the tempering, heat the pure ghee in a small skillet and fry the onions until they are light brown. Add the tomatoes, garlic paste, and ginger and cook for 2 minutes, stirring continuously. Add the cinnamon, pepper, black cardamom, bay leaves, and cloves and continue to stir. Lastly add the turmeric, green chiles, and ground coriander and cook for a further 2 minutes. Add this tempering to the mashed dals and chicken.

Squeeze the juice from 2 of the lemons and stir it into the Chicken Haleem.

Garnish with the mint leaves, fried onion slices, red chiles, and lemon wedges, and serve hot.

Haleem goes well with very crisp tandoori rotis.

GOAN FISH CURRY

milk from 1 large coconut
1 teaspoon sugar
3 pomfrets, roughly 10in long,
    filleted and sliced into
    1½in pieces
2oz tamarind, soaked in 2
    tablespoons water for 20
    minutes and sieved
salt to taste

FOR THE TEMPERING
3 tablespoons vegetable oil
2 tablespoons black
    mustard seeds
8–10 curry leaves
3 green chiles, slit lengthways
    and seeded

serves 6

FOR THE CURRY PASTE
1 large coconut, shredded and
    mashed to a paste with a
    little water
10–12 black peppercorns
6–8 dried Kashmiri red chiles,
    freshly ground (or a good
    brand of chili powder)
1 tablespoon ground coriander
10–12 garlic cloves, peeled
1 tablespoon sesame seeds
1¼in piece of fresh ginger root,
    peeled and roughly chopped

In India the head and tail of the fish are cooked with the fillets but this is optional. If you cannot find pomfrets, any other firm-fleshed white fish such as cod or monkfish will work. Get the fish merchant to fillet the fish for you.

Grind together the ingredients for the curry paste. Add it to the coconut milk. Pour the mixture into a small saucepan and bring to a boil over a medium heat. Cook for 10–12 minutes.

Tip this mixture into a large saucepan and add the sugar, some salt, and the fish pieces. Cook over a medium heat for 5 minutes, stirring gently from time to time. Stir in the sieved tamarind water.

Heat the oil in a small skillet and add the mustard seeds, curry leaves, and green chiles. Cook on a high heat, stirring continuously to prevent burning. When they turn brown add them to the curry. Serve with short-grained rice or brown rice.

Junglee Mutton

4oz pure ghee (see page 155)
2 onions, sliced
6–8 garlic cloves, peeled
   and halved
3oz dried Kashmiri red chiles,
   halved and seeded (or other
   good quality dried chiles)
2¼lbs mutton, taken from the leg
   and cut into 1½–2in cubes
salt to taste

serves 6

The name of this dish reflects its origins. After a royal hunt, the maharajas and their entourage would be served this in the jungle. The taste of the mutton is enhanced by the hot chiles that were easy to carry on such hunts.

In a large saucepan, heat the pure ghee and fry the onions over a high heat, stirring continuously. Add the garlic just before they turn dark brown. Add the dried red chiles and continue cooking for 3 minutes.

Add the mutton and keep stirring to prevent burning. When the meat has browned, reduce the heat and add some salt and 2 cups of water. Cover with a lid and seal the pan with dough (see page 38). Continue cooking on a low heat for 45 minutes. When the lid is opened, the water should have evaporated leaving flaming red mutton.

Serve hot, with soft chapattis.

Yakhni Pulao

MUTTON AND RICE PILAF

9oz ghee (see page 155)
4 large onions, 2 ground to a smooth
   paste, 2 finely sliced
6–8 garlic cloves, peeled and
   ground to a smooth paste
2¼lbs mutton, cut into 1½–2in pieces
18oz basmati rice, soaked in cold
   water for 30 minutes
salt to taste

FOR THE YAKHNI (IN
SECURLEY TIED
CHEESECLOTH BAG)
1 cinnamon stick
6 cloves
10 black peppercorns
3 bay leaves
1 tablespoon cumin seeds
2 tablespoons coriander seeds

A yakhni is a cheesecloth pouch in which herbs and spices are kept during cooking, so that they can be discarded easily after they have released their flavors. Indian cuisine reached great heights of refinement at the courts of the Awadhi rulers during the eighteenth and nineteenth centuries. Of the range of pulaos created there, the mildest and most subtle was the yakhni pulao. Ram Prasad, the Kapoors' cook, learnt this recipe from the great master cook of the old Kapoor home.

Heat 7oz of the ghee in a large saucepan, add the onion paste and garlic paste and fry for 3–4 minutes, taking care not to let them burn. Add the mutton and cook over a low heat until lightly browned, stirring continuously to prevent burning. Pour in 3½ pints of water and tuck in the yakhni, and add some salt. Cover the pan and simmer over gentle heat for around 1 hour. When the mutton is tender, remove the yakhni from the liquor and, once it is cool enough to handle, squeeze it to drain the last bit of flavor back into the pan before discarding the pouch.

In a small skillet, heat the remaining ghee and fry the sliced onions over a high heat until they are dark brown. Set aside for the garnish.

Strain the liquor from the mutton into a separate pan and keep the mutton warm. Add the soaked rice to the liquor and cook, covered, on a low heat until the water has been absorbed and the rice is cooked but firm. Then gently mix in the mutton.

Serve hot, garnished with the sliced browned onions.

serves 6

SANGAM
TECHNICOLOR

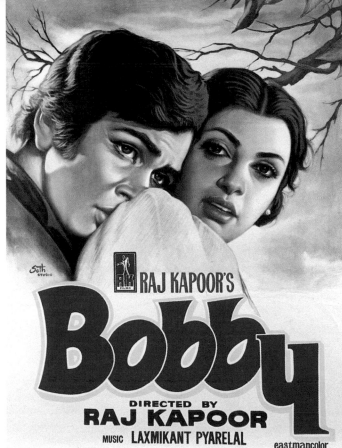

Seth STUDIO

RK FILMS

RAJ KAPOOR'S

Bobby

DIRECTED BY
RAJ KAPOOR

MUSIC LAXMIKANT PYARELAL   eastmancolor

PRINTED BY ORIENTAL OFFSET & LITHO WORKS, BOMBAY 7

Paya

TROTTERS SOUP

12 trotters, washed and scrubbed in
   hot water. Kid, goat or lamb is
   preferred but pigs' are equally
   good (if the trotters are hairy, singe
   them on open flame)
1½in piece of fresh ginger root,
   peeled and finely sliced
2 tablespoons black peppercorns
6 cloves
5 black cardamom pods
3 bay leaves
1 cinnamon stick
¼ cup cheap rice, wrapped in a
   cheesecloth
salt to taste

FOR THE TEMPERING
2 tablespoons vegetable oil
5 large onions, shredded
2 tablespoons tomato paste
1 tablespoon ginger-garlic paste
   (see page 155)
1 teaspoon red chili powder

serves 6

In the days of Raj Kapoor, the Kapoor home had the most elaborate spread of meats. This dish is unusual as it is rarely made in homes today. It originates from Central Asia, where in winter paya would be cooked on slow fires all through the night and eaten for breakfast with breads. The Moghuls made a few modifications and it was very popular as it was believed to have aphrodisiac qualities. This recipe is a more modern version and a big favorite with Rishi Kapoor.

Put the trotters, ginger, and all the spices in a large saucepan, cover with 6¼ pints of water and bring to a boil on a high heat. Season with salt and place the rice pack in the center. Cover the pan and simmer gently for about 2 hours until tender. Remove the rice pack and discard. Stir the soup. This can also be made in a pressure cooker, in which case reduce the quantity of water to 5¼ pints and cook for 45 minutes.

In a separate skillet, heat the oil and fry the onions until dark brown. Add the remaining ingredients and stir until the oil leaves the sides. Stir the tempering into the soup and simmer for a further 15 minutes.

Serve hot with bread. In Mumbai, paya is traditionally accompanied by brun pao (a hard bread with a soft center).

Saif Ali Khan is the eldest child of Sharmila Tagore, a glamorous actress of the 1960s and now head of the Film Censor Board, and former Indian cricket captain Mansoor Ali Pataudi. Saif studied in England, first at Lockers Park School and then Winchester College where he majored in English literature and art history. He is a keen reader, devouring anything from nineteenth century English authors like Jane Austen and the Brontë sisters to Ayn Rand. He has recently become interested in writings on African safaris and hunting stories of the 1920s. He loves to play the guitar and even hoped to be a rock star when he was younger, before acting consumed his life. His passion for music and dance shines through his performances at stage shows and on camera.

Saif Ali Khan

Saif had a steady career in Bollywood during the 1990s, then in 2001 *Dil Chahta Hai* became a huge success and turned his life around overnight. His character, Sameer, was one that audiences could relate to and really warm to. Sameer is a guy in love with the idea of love, who wears his heart on his sleeve, and Saif portrayed him with such intelligence and warmth that he outshone the rest of the cast. His next films got better and built on his success. *Kal Ho Naa Ho* (2003), *Hum Tum* (2004), for which he won the National Award for Best Actor, and then his piece de resistance, *Parineeta* (2005), in which he positively glowed. More recently his English film, *Being Cyrus* (2005), was critically praised and garnered rave reviews.

In the early days of his career, his close resemblance to his mother was a disadvantage for him. His features were considered to be too feminine by traditional Bollywood standards. Over the years he has developed a strict exercise regime and has built his body to a toned yet lithe level, that has helped him overcome that mental barrier. Today he looks a personification of the cool, well-heeled cosmopolitan Indian. His acting proficiency enables him to take on a diverse range of roles. The best directors are vying to work with him from mainstream cinema as well as alternative art house. Two of his new films are being directed by Vishal Bharadwaj: *Omkara* (2006), an adaptation of Shakespeare's *Othello*, and *Mr Mehta and Mrs Singh* (2006) with Kareena Kapoor. It's a good time to be Saif Ali Khan in Bollywood.

"My mom's food is really good—she cooks both Bengali and Mughlai cuisines extremely well. Rosa (my girlfriend) does nice Italian food." His tastes show a love of European food. In London, he likes Maggie Jones for its English food and cosy atmosphere, and Signor Sassi for Italian fare. Chinese and Japanese cuisines also feature regularly when he dines out, especially Nobu in London and Golden Dragon at the Taj Mahal, Mumbai.

Bhindi Do Piaza

OKRA WITH ONIONS

750g okra
3 tablespoons vegetable oil
5 onions, quartered
5cm piece of fresh ginger, peeled and cut
    into julienne strips
2 teaspoons cumin seeds
1 teaspoon onion seeds
6 whole green chillies
2 teaspoons ground coriander
1 teaspoon turmeric
2 teaspoons red chilli powder
salt to taste

serves 6

This is a simple and quick dish to make. Though Saif prefers meat dishes, okra is one of his favourite vegetables. Mohan Sharma, his cook, gave us this recipe. Always check the freshness of okra before buying them – they should be firm and not bendy.

Wash and pat dry the okra. Remove the stalks and slice the okra lengthways.

In a large pan, heat the oil and sauté the onions, ginger and cumin and onion seeds. Add the green chillies and the okra. Continue to sauté on a low heat, stirring frequently, for about 10 minutes. The okra should be just tender and retain a bit of bite. Stir in the ground coriander, turmeric and chilli powder. Finally stir in the salt.

Serve hot. This dish goes well with a dal and rotis and papads.

Nargisi Kofte

MEAT BALLS IN THICK GRAVY

FOR THE KOFTE

1¼lbs ground meat (lamb or chicken)
3 medium potatoes, boiled and peeled
1¼in piece of fresh ginger root, finely
   chopped
6 garlic cloves, finely chopped
2 green chiles, seeded and finely
   chopped
1 teaspoon garam masala
   (see page 154)
small bunch of cilantro, finely chopped
10 cashew nuts
2 tablespoons raisins
vegetable oil, for frying
salt to taste

FOR THE PASTE

4 onions, sliced
15 cashew nuts
4 tablespoons poppy seeds

FOR THE GRAVY

3 tablespoons ghee (see page 155)
4 large tomatoes, skinned and puréed
1 tablespoon ginger paste
   (see page 155)
1 tablespoon garlic paste
   (see page 155)
2 bay leaves
1 cinnamon stick, about 2in long
3 green cardamom pods
2 teaspoons Kashmiri chili powder
   (or good quality chili powder)
2 teaspoons ground coriander
½ tablespoon turmeric
2 teaspoons garam masala
   (see page 154)
3 tablespoons light cream

serves 6

This dish, from the traditions of the Awadhi rulers, is Saif Ali Khan's favorite and he cooks it often. His cook Mohan Sharma, who gave this recipe, also makes a vegetarian version, replacing the meat with paneer (fresh cottage cheese).

It is common to come across recipes for Nargisi Kofte that use boiled eggs but this recipe is the authentic one, as the nawabs of the eighteenth and nineteenth centuries ate the dish.

Put the ground meat in a bowl and mash in the boiled potatoes until evenly mixed. Add the chopped ginger, garlic, and green chiles and mix well. Add some salt and the garam masala and mix thoroughly, then add the finely chopped cilantro. Divide into six portions and mold into balls using the palms of your hand. Mix the cashew nuts and raisins together and divide into six portions. Make a hole in the center of each meatball, add the cashew-raisin mix and close up the hole. This is a raw "kofta."

Heat the oil in a large skillet and fry the kofte on all sides until golden brown. Set aside and keep warm.

To make the paste, put the onions, cashews, and poppy seeds in a saucepan and cover with ¾ cup of water. Bring to a boil and simmer for 10 minutes. Leave to cool, then blend in a food processor.

To make the gravy, heat the ghee in a saucepan and add the onion and the cashew and poppy seed paste. Cook until the oil separates at the sides of the paste, stirring continuously. Add the tomato purée, ginger and garlic pastes and continue cooking, stirring, for 2 minutes. Add the remaining spices and keep stirring. Lastly pour in the cream and stir well.

Place the fried kofte in the gravy and cook over a low heat for 3 minutes to warm them through.

Serve hot, with rotis and a fresh salad.

(For the vegetarian version, follow the recipe substituting fresh paneer for the ground meat and add 2 tablespoons of cornstarch to bind the paneer.)

The eldest son of the handsome actor Vinod Khanna, Rahul Khanna is charming and soft-spoken, with a sensitive manner and a languid quality that make his performances on screen seem effortless. Perhaps his many years of being a VJ on MTV-Asia have provided a sense of ease in front of the camera.

Rahul grew up in Mumbai. He recalls the mango season that always had a festive feel, with friends competing with each other to see how many could be devoured in a sitting. It was a carefree time, when being mussed up with mango juice streaming down your face wasn't frowned upon. "Now I can only eat it sliced and diced" he sighs. The family had a beach house and Rahul recalls a mangosteen-like fruit that grew nearby called a targola that he loved. He remembers climbing mulberry trees for their fruit and loving the smell and bite of green mangoes.

Rahul Khanna

Thinking back to his younger days, Rahul recollects carrying pounds of raw mutton on a nine-hour drive from Thimphu, the capital of Bhutan, to a place up in the mountains where his uncle was stationed. He spent his vacation eating the meat as stews and soups with fresh breads. "It's amazing how sense memories work—even today when I have certain dishes, all these memories rush in. Some of my most spectacular memories come from the Parsi weddings and Navjots (a Parsi celebratory feast). The food is served for hours over many courses on banana leaves with that dreadfully sweet red raspberry drink which we loved as kids."

Work has taken Rahul away from Mumbai to two cities that are food heavens—Singapore and New York. His Punjabi and Parsi taste buds have found an explosion of flavors there that widened his culinary experiences:

"New York is a gastronomic smorgasbord—it was there that my palate became refined. I had friends there who really broadened my culinary horizons, for example the world of cheese just opened up. When I was growing up, a slab of Kraft cheese was really living it up. Then I sampled the cheeses in New York—fresh, young, aged, soft, hard, goat and sheep cheeses, with rind and without...I loved them all. I used to live next to the 9th Avenue cheese market. It's a gourmet's heaven. I would pick up most of my meals there. I also loved Jean Georges' restaurant. The nouvelle cuisine was all the rage there ten years back—I simply loved the wonderful combinations; pan-seared fish with fruits, black pepper ice cream, chocolates with chiles...this sense and ability to combine unconventional elements into a dish. I realized food is an art form

while living there and it's something that has stayed with me."

Singapore too left its culinary footprints: "My favorite restaurant there was a local one in a government housing block and you would never guess such good food happened there. It's called Hua Zhu: they make the most wonderful fresh crabs with black pepper, shrimp with dried red chiles, steamed local vegetables, Chinese breads, and deep-fried baby squid."

While Rahul's sense for good food is keen, he does not cook himself. For him the pleasure is in collecting different and exciting food experiences and being the connoisseur and raconteur of his many adventures.

above: Rahul Khanna has been a selective actor. His first film, *1947: Earth* (1999), got him the Best Newcomer Filmfare Award. He is a voracious reader and has a passion for collecting recipes!

Paneer Masala

FRESH COTTAGE CHEESE MASALA

18oz soft paneer
4 tablespoons vegetable oil
1 tablespoon cumin seeds
6 large onions, finely diced
3 large tomatoes, skinned and chopped
1 teaspoon tandoori chat masala
 (optional, see page 154)
salt to taste

serves 6

This simple dish can be made in no time at all.

Cut the paneer into cubes or slices. Heat the oil in a skillet and fry the paneer cubes until golden brown on all sides. Remove from the pan, drain on paper towels and keep warm.

Add the cumin seeds to the oil in the pan, followed by the onions. Fry until light brown, then add the tomatoes. Season with salt and chaat masala. Add the fried paneer pieces and continue cooking for 1 minute, stirring.

Serve hot, as an accompaniment to roti and dal or rice and dal.

SMOKED DAL

4oz mung beans (moong dal)
½ cup yellow lentils (toor dal)
1 teaspoon turmeric
2 tablespoons vegetable oil
1 tablespoon black mustard seeds
2 teaspoons cumin seeds
5–6 curry leaves
5 garlic cloves, finely chopped
1 large onion, finely chopped
1 large tomato, skinned and diced
½ tablespoon green chili pickle
 (optional)
1 tablespoon mango pickle
1 tablespoon mango chutney
salt to taste
coal, for burning

serves 6

This is a tangy dal with an unusual flavor.

In a large saucepan, mix the dals and pour in 4 cups of water. Add the turmeric and some salt and cook until they swell and turn to a smooth soup. (Dal when boiled usually forms a layer of froth on top that should be removed with a spoon.)

In a small saucepan, heat the oil. Add the mustard and cumin seeds and curry leaves. As they begin to splutter, add the chopped garlic and onion and fry until light brown. Add the tomato and, when the oil separates from the sides of the tomatoes, stir the mix into the cooked dal. Add the pickles and chutney and stir.

Take a burning coal (use a lump of barbecue charcoal heated over a flame until it is red hot) and place it in a steel bowl with some vegetable oil at the bottom. It will begin to smoke. Put the bowl in the center of the pan containing the dal and cover the dal pan tightly. Leave for 20 minutes or so to let the smoke penetrate the dal and only open the pan when you are ready to serve.

Serve hot. This dal can be served as a main course as it is particularly flavorful. It goes well with rice and rotis.

Bhindi Fry

CRISPY OKRA

18oz okra
4 tablespoons vegetable oil
5 curry leaves
2 tablespoons mustard seeds
2 tablespoons green mango powder
 (amchoor)
salt

serves 6

Amchoor is prepared from green mangoes that are sun-dried and powdered. Okra needs to be fresh—avoid bendy and tired-looking specimens as they are often slimy!

Wash the okra and pat dry. Cut into medium-sized pieces and sprinkle with salt. Set aside to sweat for 10 minutes or so. Heat half the oil and fry the okra until dark and crispy. Keep the heat high and continue stirring. Transfer to a serving dish and keep warm.

In the remaining oil, fry the curry leaves and mustard seeds until they pop. Pour them with the oil over the okra. Dust with mango powder and serve hot with roti, dal, and yogurt.

Dahi Vada

WHITE LENTIL PUFFS IN YOGURT

FOR THE VADAS
1½ cups white lentils (split and skinned black lentils)
pinch of baking soda
vegetable oil for deep-frying
salt to taste

FOR THE YOGURT MIX
18oz plain yogurt
1 tablespoon cumin seeds, roasted and ground
2 tablespoons red chili powder
2 tablespoons granulated sugar

FOR THE TAMARIND CHUTNEY
7oz tamarind, seeded and soaked in 1 cup water for 30 minutes
¼ cup jaggery or soft brown sugar

serves 6

This is a savory dish that was originally one of the snacks that traveling vendors sold in the late afternoon.

Thoroughly wash the dal and soak them in water for a minimum of 12 hours. The water level should be 1¼ins above the dal. Grind to a thick paste with the water. Season with some salt and add a pinch of baking soda to the paste.

Heat some oil in a wok for deep-frying. Spoon out the mixture as dumplings into the hot oil, reduce the heat and cook till golden brown and crisp. Remove and cool the vadas on paper towels. Once cool, soak them in water for 5 minutes and then gently squeeze the water out.

Blend the yogurt to a smooth consistency with the cumin, chili powder, and sugar. Make the chutney by blending the tamarind with the jaggery and sieve.

Place the vadas in a serving dish and pour the yogurt mix over them. Top with tamarind chutney. Refrigerate for 15 minutes and serve cool.

BOHRI CHICKEN CURRY

2in piece of fresh ginger root, peeled and roughly chopped
4–6 garlic cloves, peeled
2–3 green chiles, slit lengthways and seeded
3½lbs boneless chicken (leg or breast) skinned and cut into small pieces
4 tablespoons vegetable oil
1 cup coconut milk
juice of 4 tomatoes
salt to taste

FOR THE BOHRI PASTE
3oz roasted chickpeas (unsalted)
2oz semolina
2oz sesame seeds
3oz cashew nuts
¾oz coriander seeds

serves 6

Rahul loves home-cooked Indian food and Sunita, their cook, makes a great Bohri Chicken Curry. Originally, the Bohris were a Muslim trading community.

First make a paste by blending the ginger, garlic, and chiles in a food-processor. Coat the chicken pieces with the paste and leave to marinate for 15 minutes in a cool place.

Meanwhile make the Bohri paste. Whizz all the ingredients, together with 3 tablespoons of water, in a food-processor until smooth. Heat the oil in a large saucepan and fry the Bohri paste for few minutes until it turns light brown.

Add the chicken pieces to the pan along with some salt and a little water to prevent burning. Simmer over a low heat for 20 minutes or until the chicken is cooked. Then stir in the coconut milk and tomato juice and bring to a boil. Serve hot, with rotis or rice.

Manisha Koirala, with her fair skin and expressive eyes, is a consummate and passionate actress, and many of her performances remain unrivaled. *Bombay* (1995), *Khamoshi* (1996), and *Dil Se* (1998), demonstrate her ability to live and breathe her characters. She is the *ek ladki ko dekha toh aisa lagaa*—the ideal, romantic, ethereal fantasy figure. She continues to explore the world of cinema by training in film direction at a college in New York, while back home in India she runs a film production company.

Manisha is also a true food enthusiast. A connoisseur of fine eating and haute cuisine, she will not hesitate to enjoy regular "unit food" (meals served during film shoots and often a shade too oily and heavily spiced). When she talks of food, you can see her passion. Her eyes sparkle with memories and she can taste the dishes all over again.

Manisha Koirala

She cooks like a dream because, she believes, "I express my love through food." Her friends talk excitedly of the exquisite meals she has made for them with her trademark flair and acute sense of combinations. Anyone that has sampled her food can tell you how instinctively she relates to her ingredients.

Growing up in Benares (now Varanasi), Manisha was an athletic child who loved basketball and her daadi's (paternal grandmother's) cooking. The family enjoyed their mealtimes and they would always eat together. There was a sense of perfection, she recalls, in her daadi's food and cooking style. The food was a mix of North Indian and Nepali cuisines. Everybody in her home cooked. "Our celebration and togetherness came from cooking and we loved feeding others and each other."

Her career and travels have provided her with an appreciation of food from around the globe, and she seems to intuitively relate to classical French cuisine. "They pour a certain passion in their cooking," she says with gleaming eyes. She also enjoys Japanese at Nobu in New York and waxes lyrical about ethnic Indian cuisine—she has a special fondness for southern spicy dishes and Gujarati thaalis.

opposite page: Manisha joined Bollywood as a young teenager. Apart from her ethereal looks and immense talent, she is also an accomplished Bharat Natyam and Manipuri dancer.

Her food experiences continue to expand and she loves trying out new restaurants. Mangi Ferra, a stylish Italian restaurant in Juhu, Mumbai, has introduced her to the thin crust pizzas cooked in mango wood-fired ovens, and she now can't get enough of them. She is a fan of the butter garlic crab at Trishna in Fort Bombay and she even introduced fondue to the general manager at the Taj Coromandal, who put it straight on the menu! She is clearly a woman of culture and refined tastes.

Patra Ni Macchi

FISH STEAMED IN BANANA LEAVES

12 large pomfret fillets, or any firm
   white fish
5–6 banana leaves, or aluminum foil
3 tablespoons vinegar or red
   wine vinegar

FOR THE CHUTNEY
1½ fresh coconuts, shredded
5 green chiles, seeded
a large handful of cilantro leaves
a large handful of mint leaves
2 small onions
2 garlic cloves, peeled
1 in piece of fresh ginger root, peeled
1 tablespoon cumin seeds, roasted
1 tablespoon sugar
5–6 tablespoons lime juice
salt to taste

serves 6

Manisha believes that her friend and "food confidante" Parvana Boga Noorani, is the best chef and hostess of Parsi food she has ever come across. The following Parsi dishes are her recipes.

Put all the ingredients for the chutney except the lime juice in a food-processor and add 1 tablespoon of water. Whizz for 2 minutes, then add the lime juice so that the flavor is slightly spicy, sweet, and sour.

Wash the fish and pat dry.

Remove the center stalk from the banana leaves and cut into 12 large pieces. Pass the leaves quickly over a flame to soften them.

Coat each slice of fish liberally with the chutney and place each on a piece of banana leaf. Fold the leaf over and tie up with a string to completely seal in the fish. (If you find that the leaf does not completely enclose the fish, use an extra piece of banana leaf to close the gap.)

Heat some water in a steamer and add the vinegar. When the steam rises, place the fish wraps on the top, cover and cook for 20 minutes.

Serve hot, with freshly made roti or plain dal and rice.

Gor Amli Kachumber

SWEET AND SOUR RELISH

2 onions, thinly sliced
7oz dates, mashed to a pulp
7oz tamarind, strings and
    seeds removed
½ cup jaggery or soft
    brown sugar
1 teaspoon chili powder
½ teaspoon ground cumin
2 tablespoons cilantro leaves,
    chopped
1 green chili, seeded and
    finely chopped
salt to taste

serves 6

This kachumber is quite different from the usual Indian relish and is a mandatory accompaniment to the dhansak feast. There will be enough relish for 3 separate feasts when you have made this recipe; it can be kept refrigerated, in an airtight jar, for 2 weeks.

Sprinkle the onion slices with 1 teaspoon of salt and leave them to sweat for 2 minutes; then rinse them in 3½ tablespoons of warm water. This allows the onions to get a little salty and removes their sharpness.

Pour 1 cup of water in a saucepan and add the dates, tamarind, jaggary, chili powder, and ground cumin. Bring to a boil, reduce the heat and simmer for 5–10 minutes. Remove from the heat, strain and cool. Measure out one cup and add to it the onions, the chopped cilantro and green chiles.

Serve cool.

BROWN RICE

18oz basmati rice
2 tablespoons ghee
  (see page 155)
1 small onion, finely chopped
2 cinnamon sticks
8 cloves
8 black peppercorns
4 large whole black cardamoms
2 bay leaves
1 teaspoon cumin seeds
1 teaspoon sugar
salt to taste

serves 8

This rice is a common accompaniment to the Parsi dhansak feast.

Wash the rice thoroughly and soak it in water for 30 minutes. Drain well and set aside.

Heat the ghee in a saucepan large enough to hold the rice. Add the onions and fry until just translucent. Add the cinnamon, cloves, peppercorns, black cardamoms, and bay leaves. Continue to cook until the onions are golden brown, then stir in the cumin seeds and sugar and cook until the sugar caramelizes. Add the drained rice to the pan and stir well so that all the grains of rice are coated with ghee. Add 2½ pints of hot water and salt to taste.

Cover the pan and cook on low heat until all the water has been absorbed and the rice is tender.

Serve hot as an accompaniment.

Dhansak Dal

SPICED LENTILS WITH MUTTON

18oz lamb or mutton
1 cup yellow lentils (arhar or toor dal)
½ cup split red lentils (masoor dal)
4oz split mung beans (moong dal)
3 tablespoons ginger-garlic paste
   (see page 155)
2 tablespoons mint leaves
3 bunches small fenugreek leaves,
   chopped
1 medium eggplant, chopped
4oz red pumpkin, chopped
2 onions, chopped
2 potatoes, peeled and quartered
6 black peppercorns
½ teaspoon turmeric
salt to taste

FOR THE TEMPERING

3 tablespoons peanut oil or ghee
1 large onion, finely chopped
4 tablespoons dhansak masala
   (see page 154)
4 tablespoons sambhar masala
   (see page 154)
1 tablespoon garam masala
   (see page 154)
3 large ripe tomatoes, skinned
   and chopped

serves 6

This is one of the most popular Parsi dishes.

Wash the meat and cut it into 1 ¼ inch cubes—use meat with bones in and have the butcher cut it for you, as the bones add flavor. In a large saucepan add the meat and all the other ingredients except those for the tempering. Cover with water and bring to a boil. Remove any froth that comes to the surface, reduce the heat and simmer for 45–50 minutes until the lentils are just tender and the meat is cooked through.

Remove the meat pieces and keep them warm in a low oven. Pass the remaining mixture through a mouli or a strainer to purée the dal and vegetables and then return the meat to the puréed vegetables.

Heat the oil or ghee in a saucepan and fry the onion until lightly browned. Add the powdered spices and cook, stirring well, until the oil rises to the surface. Sprinkle with a little water if required.

Add the tomatoes and mix well. Continue cooking on a low heat, stirring occasionally, until the tomatoes turn to a smooth paste.

Purée this masala mixture and add it to the dal and lamb. Bring to a boil to blend the flavors.

Serve hot with brown rice (see page 92), kabobs (see page 94), pieces of fried Bombay duck (a traditional accompaniment), and gor amli kachumber (see page 92).

Kebabs

9oz ground lamb or mutton
2 tablespoons ginger-garlic paste (see page 155)
½ tablespoon sambhar masala (see page 154)
1 tablespoon dhansak masala (see page 154)
1 cup mashed potatoes
1 large onion, finely chopped

2 tablespoons chopped cilantro leaves
2–3 tablespoons chopped mint
1 green chile, chopped
½ teaspoon powdered mace
2 eggs, lightly beaten
about ½ pint vegetable or groundnut oil
salt to taste

serves 6

These taste great with dhanksak dal (see page 93).

Mix the ground meat with the ginger-garlic paste and the two masalas and marinate overnight.

Add the mashed potatoes, onion, cilantro, mint, chile, mace, and some salt and mix well. Pour in the eggs and mix in. Shape into walnut-sized balls and deep-fry in hot oil until golden brown.

Serve hot.

Rang De Basanti, Rakeysh Mehra's second film as a director and producer, is engaging and filled with a certain mood and energy that is refreshing in Bollywood. The film clearly made a connection with its audiences and was 2006's most vibrant film. Rakeysh has shown his desire and ability to break the Bollywood mold. He has also demonstrated with all his films a technical sharpness and awareness no doubt acquired from ten years spent making advertising films.

Rakeysh was born into a world filled with food. His father worked as the head of Food and Beverages at Claridge's hotel in New Delhi. His father, affectionately called "Bauji," came from a North-West frontier province in Pakistan. When the family started a restaurant, it was called Bauji Ka Dhaba and it served a mix of North-West Frontier, Lucknow, and Hyderabadi cuisines.

Rakeysh Mehra

"Something interesting about Indian cuisine is that it is not restricted by recipes. It's more about what is available and how to combine it. I cannot relate to structured cooking…it's more, 'let's see what we can do with what is here.' I have never used a recipe book. I would rather meet the grandmothers and learn from them."

Rakeysh loves to spend time in the kitchen experimenting, having learnt the art from both his father and his mother. "India is so enigmatic when it comes to food. In the smallest of villages you will eat the best of dishes." One of his most memorable meals was in a small Ladhaki village where he ate meat dumplings with sticky rice and ground chili that had a totally unique flavor. This was washed down with a refreshing rice brew called chaang. "I kept eating for four hours, listening to stories of the Chinese war around a campfire while my host's wife and daughter just kept cooking for us. Another time, in Himachal Pradesh, I got caught in a flash flood and ended up eating the best rajma-chawal (kidney beans and rice). The women kept cooking the dish all day long, adding fresh material to the old so that the dish never really finished!" It is such rustic, earthy food, inspired by memories, that beckon Rakeysh's taste buds.

On a recent trip to Cambodia he discovered a country suffering from a long war and struggle. Rather than visit places recommended by his travel guide, he chose to take an off-road into the deep interiors, where he met and socialized with the communities he found there and ate local food. "The food was a revelation—shrimp and vegetables cooked with local sauces. I did the same thing in Jaisalmer, exploring the food of the interior desert. I am more interested in how food evolves; the nuances of the environment and state of mind while cooking. I think Bengali food is really interesting—it's simple to make, but the flavors always come alive."

Rakeysh has eaten in the finest restaurants in many cities around the world, but he feels there is often a forced stylization to the food and cooking methods he is presented with. "I do not reject the elaborations of haute cuisine but I think the art of cooking gets diluted." Instead, he relishes the food of the locals as it is stripped of unnecessary ornamentation and the natural flavors are allowed to emerge, creating a unique and far more satisfying taste and experience.

right: Rakeysh Mehra is at heart an explorer of rugged terrains. He loves to seek the adventure of the lesser traveled roads both in India and elsewhere and observe the world with a quiet mind.

below: Rakeysh Mehra directs Aamir Khan and Soha Ali Khan during the filming of *Rang De Basanti* (2006) at Amritsar. The film became both a commercial and cult hit with younger audiences.

Thukpa

LADAKHI NOODLE SOUP

11oz egg noodles
6 tablespoons vegetable oil
2in piece of fresh ginger root, peeled and
  cut into julienne strips
8 garlic cloves, chopped
18oz ground lamb
2 onions, thinly sliced
1 cabbage, shredded finely
2 tablespoons soy sauce
a large handful of chopped cilantro
salt to taste

serves 6

Rakeysh visited the Himalayan desert region of Ladakh during a film location recce. He met Odpal George, a local scout and good cook, who sent these recipes with a note: "We spent more time cooking, eating and talking about food than recceing!" On a cold day, a thukpa is the most envigorating meal. Lamb is most often used in this dish but it can also be made with kid, beef, or pork.

In a large saucepan, bring 4 cups of salted water to a boil and add the noodles. Reduce the heat and simmer for 7–8 minutes or until cooked. Drain and spread them on a large tray or work surface or place in a bowl. Pour 4 tablespoons of the oil over them and stir with chopsticks or a fork to coat them well.

Heat the remaining oil in a large saucepan and stir-fry the ginger and garlic for 2 minutes, then add the ground meat. Keep stirring regularly until the meat is almost cooked. This could take up to 30 minutes. Add the onions and cabbage and cook for a further 4–5 minutes, then pour in 4 cups of water and the soy sauce. Bring to a boil, stir in the noodles and add salt if needed.

Ladle the thukpa and noodles into warmed bowls and garnish with chopped cilantro. Or it can also be served by placing the noodles in a bowl and pouring the thukpa over them. This dish is best when piping hot.

Momos (see page 101) make a good accompaniment.

Kabargah

KASHMIRI LAMB CHOP

18oz three-rib lamb chops with 2 bones removed
1¾ cups milk
1 bay leaf
1 teaspoon aniseed
1 tablespoon black peppercorns
1 teaspoon red chili powder
4 whole green cardamoms
2 cloves

FOR THE BATTER
2 eggs, beaten
14oz plain yogurt
1 tablespoon red chili powder
1oz cornstarch
⅓ cup ghee (see page 155)
salt to taste

FOR BASTING
¼ teaspoon saffron soaked in a tablespoon of milk
⅓ cup ghee (if using a tandoor)

FOR THE GARNISH
mint leaves

serves 6

This is an adaptation of a popular Kashmiri recipe and served at Bauji Ka Dhaba, the Mehra family's restaurant. Rajan Mehra, Rakeysh's brother, shared the recipe. As with other authentic slow-cooked meats, this dish takes some 3+ hours to prepare. If barbecuing the chops, you will need 6 metal skewers.

Ask the butcher to prepare the chops for you. Wash and pat them dry.

In a large saucepan put the milk, bay leaf, aniseed, peppercorns, chili powder, cardamoms, and cloves, cover with 1 cup of water and add the chops. Bring to a boil and then cook on a low heat, just simmering. Once the liquid dries up, add salt and set aside for 20 minutes.

Mix ingredients for the batter. Coat the chops well and leave to marinate for 1 hour in a cool place.

Oil the skewers and thread the chops onto them. Place on a hot barbecue and grill for 15–20 minutes, turning once, until the lamb is cooked to your taste. Baste them well from time to time during the cooking with the saffron milk. (Alternatively, cook in a preheated oven at 350°F for 30–40 minutes.)

Or, put into a hot tandoor and cook for 5 minutes. Remove and baste the kabobs with melted ghee followed by saffron milk. Put the chops back in the tandoor for a further 5 minutes.

Serve hot, with green mint leaves and chutney.

Momos

GROUND MEAT DUMPLINGS WITH HOT SAUCE

FOR THE FILLING
18oz ground lamb or goat
2oz mutton fat or dripping
4 large onions, finely chopped
3 tablespoons ginger-garlic paste
(see page 155)
a large handful of chopped cilantro
salt to taste

FOR THE DUMPLINGS
6 cups all-purpose flour
1 teaspoon salt

FOR THE HOT SAUCE
1 onion, finely chopped
2 large tomatoes, chopped
4 tablespoons red chili flakes
3 tablespoons vegetable oil
1¼in piece of fresh ginger root, peeled and
finely chopped
8 garlic cloves, finely chopped
a large handful of chopped cilantro
salt to taste

**serves 6 (makes approximately
24 momos)**

In Ladakh there is a special steamer for momos called a motko but most regular steamers work equally well as long as there are separators so that the dumplings do not stick to each other. This recipe also comes from Odpal George. Traditionally the meat, either lamb or goat, would be chopped by hand rather than put through a grinder—it gives the dish a better texture.

Mix together the ground meat, fat, onions, ginger-garlic paste, and cilantro and season well with salt.

Next, make the dumplings by mixing the flour and salt with about ⅓ cup of water into a medium-hard dough. Divide into 24 equal pieces and roll them into balls.

Flatten each ball with the palm of your hand and place a large helping of the spiced ground meat on each. Shape them into dumplings, enclosing the filling.

Place the raw momos in a steamer and cook for 25–30 minutes.

To make the hot sauce, put the onions, tomatoes, and red chili flakes in a heavy saucepan. Add 4 cups of water and bring to a boil, then cover, reduce the heat and simmer for 10 minutes.

In a small skillet, heat the oil and add the ginger and garlic and fry it for 2 minutes. Add them to the sauce together with the cilantro and mix well.

Serve the hot momos with hot sauce.

Raan Nawabi

THE ROYAL LEG OF LAMB

3½lbs leg of lamb
1 potato (for alternative method)
1 large onion, coarsely chopped
4 garlic cloves
1¼in piece of fresh ginger root,
    peeled and coarsely chopped
1 tablespoon black peppercorns
1 teaspoon salt

FOR THE MARINADE
3 tablespoons plain yogurt, hung in
    cheesecloth for 4 hours
2 tablespoons lemon juice
½in piece of fresh ginger root, peeled
    and shredded
2 tablespoons chopped cilantro
2 tablespoons coriander seeds,
    roasted and ground
1 tablespoon cumin seeds, roasted
    and ground
1½ teaspoons red chili powder
½ teaspoon freshly shredded nutmeg
⅓ cup canola or vegetable oil
2 teaspoons salt

TO BASTE
3–4 tablespoons ghee (see page 155)
½ teaspoon saffron strands, soaked
    in 2 tablespoons milk

FOR THE GARNISH
green mint chutney
pickled onions

serves 6

This is Rakeysh Mehra's favorite dish and his family restaurant, Bauji Ka Dhaba, has two styles of preparation of the raan. Both are given here by his brother, Rajan. The lamb should be marinated overnight or at least five hours in a cool place. Once cooked, the lamb is tender enough to be eaten with a spoon.

Wash the lamb and pat dry. Put it in a large roasting pan with the onion, garlic, ginger, peppercorns, and salt. Pour in 3 cups of water and bring to a boil, then simmer for 30 minutes and leave to cool.

Meanwhile, mix together the ingredients for the marinade. When the meat is cool enough to handle, make deep cuts all over it and rub in the marinade. Set aside overnight or for at least 5 hours.

Preheat the oven to 375°F. Roast the lamb for 1 hour, basting it with the ghee and the saffron milk every 15 minutes or so. Alternatively, skewer the leg, tie the bone to the skewer and pierce a potato through it to help hold the leg in place. Put the skewer in the tandoor for 15 minutes. Baste the leg and put it back in the tandoor until cooked.

Remove from the skewer. Decorate the bone end of the lamb with silver foil. Garnish with green mint chutney and pickled onions. This goes well with tandoori roti or naan and Kaali Dal (see page 150).

Rani Mukerji burst into the limelight and began her journey to stardom with her third film, playing Tina Malhotra, the girl who made Shah Rukh Khan's heart sing in *Kuch Kuch Hota Hai* (1998). Her energy and emotive power was compared to her cousin, Kajol, a big Bollywood star, and was a sign of the success she would soon attain. There is something distinctive about Rani—her husky voice, the convincing spontaneity, and edge of humor she brings to performances make her delightful to watch. She has the ability to make her characters feel like familiar people and she shines on screen even in small roles.

Rani Mukerji

Rani comes from a film background—her father was a producer and her grandfather created the Filmalya Studios. After *Kuch Kuch Hota Hai*, Rani played the lead in many films before she got her next box-office hit. Her portrayal of a modern girl from a lower-class family in *Saathiya* (2002) was a performance audiences really connected with and believed in. Since then she has had a string of successful films and won dozens of awards.

Female-centric films are rare in Bollywood and Rani got cast for the most unusual of them all in *Black* (2005), playing Michelle, a deaf-mute-blind girl. Amitabh Bachchan played her teacher and the pairing was inspired. Rani gave her character a certain lightness and imbued her with a positivity that displaced the morbidity of the situation. She accentuated the joy of learning and the importance of living life to the fullest. It was a hugely emotional and moving perfomance. With no songs and a strong Western stylization it broke all the boundaries but it turned out to be a successful experiment and a risk worth taking. *Time* (Europe) magazine rated it as one of the year's best films and Rani won appreciation with both popular and critical awards. That same year her film *Paheli* was selected for the Oscars. There is no doubting that Rani is, and always will be, Bollywood's sweetheart.

When she was seven, Deepti Naval decided that she would be either an actress or a nun. Bollywood would be much the poorer if she had chosen the latter. She grew up in Amritsar in a literary and artistic home, and a variety of intellectual and esthetic influences have made her multi-dimensional. Today, with over sixty films to her name, two books of poems published, and exhibitions of paintings and photography, Deepti continues to enthral and surprise, always finding new ways to express herself and the world she lives in.

Deepti Naval

Deepti started her film career with a small part in a period film *Junoon* (1978), that led to a controversial role in *Ek Baar Phir* (1980) as the traditional housewife who chose to find love with another man. Soon she was a sought-after actress in art house film circles. At the beginnning she tended to choose roles that portrayed modern liberal women and experimented with unusual themes. A natural and spontaneous actress with large warm eyes and a radiant smile, she could have become the traditional Indian heroine but she was drawn to films with much darker and more complex themes and characters. Her performances throughout her career have showcased real, intelligent, and gutsy women.

Alongside her acting career, Deepti has continued to write and paint and has also been on several treks. Her frozen river trek in Zanskar made her the first non-Ladakhi Indian woman to complete the Tchadar expedition, a treacherous terrain of incredible beauty. She is also planning leading a trekking team in Ladakh and Himachal Pradesh. The Himalayas certainly have a fascinating attraction for her.

Deepti recalls her childhood in Amritsar with affection. "Our home in Amritsar was surrounded by delightful street food. I remember the elaborate aaloo tikki (potato cutlets) sold from a big round tava. It was fascinating to watch them being punched with cooked peas on top and smothered with tamarind and mint chutney. Then the white of beaten curds on top of the red and green chutneys and finally the shredded radish and chopped green mango and onions. Just next to this seller were the aluminum cones filled with malai kulfi (handmade ice-cream) to cool the spices of the tikkis. Even today when I go to the city I indulge in Gyan Halwai's lassi (thick sweet buttermilk) to relive the magic of those days." Her move to New York as a teenager opened her eyes to a whole new world of food and completely changed her attitude towards it. One of the prime influences was a salad bar on 57th Street that had over thirty different varieties, something Deepti had never experienced before!

Her perfect skin and body are a result of a healthy-eating regimen. Her walks and exercise regime are sacrosanct and she likes to start her day with a high-protein breakfast later followed by a light lunch. Dinner is usually a salad or stir-fry. She combines fresh broccoli, spinach, yellow and red peppers, tofu, and other vegetables, lightly tossed in olive oil, with a dash of balsamic vinegar. "This and curds are my everyday foods. I also love simple dal and roti with lightly spiced vegetables cooked in minimal oil. I have a serious problem eating chiles so it's rare for me to eat the hot Indian cuisine."

Deepti's bookshelves are lined with natural and health-food books amid poetry and literature reflecting her many passions and the zest for adventure that defines her life.

opposite page: Deepti Naval as Aarti in *Saudagar* (1991) takes on the wrath of two warring families so that she can be with her lover. This film was Manisha Koirala's first film and the two actresses have been very close friends since its filming.

right: Deepti Naval played Chirutha, a woman whose father wants to sell her for dowry to the first man who can provide her with the money. Directed by Tanvir Ahmed and set in Kerala, this is one of Deepti's early art house cinema films (1981).

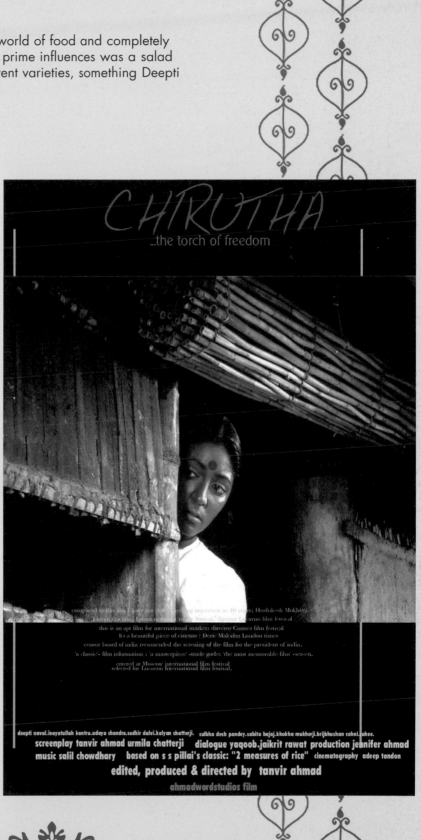

CHIRUTHA
...the torch of freedom

compared to this film I have not done anything important in 40 years: Hrishikesh Mukherji
I loved this film, I want to show it to the friends: director Locarno film festival
this is an apt film for international market: director Cannes film festival
It's a beautiful piece of cinema : Deric Malcolm London times
censor board of india recomended the screening of the film for the president of india.
'a classic'- film information : 'a masterpiece'-trade guide: 'the most memorable film'-screen.
entered at Moscow international film festival
selected for Locarno International film festival.

deepti naval.inayatullah kantru.udaya chandra.sudhir dalvi.kalyan chatterji. sulbha desh pandey.sabita bajaj.khokha mukherji.brijbhushan sahni.juhee.
screenplay tanvir ahmad urmila chatterji   **dialogue** yaqoob.jaikrit rawat **production** jennifer ahmad
music salil chowdhary   **based on** s s pillai's classic: "2 measures of rice" **cinematography** adeep tandon
edited, produced & directed by tanvir ahmad
ahmadwordstudios film

Bombay Frankie

3½ cups refined flour (maida)
6 teaspoons oil plus extra for
   greasing and frying
6 eggs
salt to taste

FOR THE STUFFING
8 potatoes, boiled and peeled
2 onions, finely chopped
2oz fresh cilantro, chopped
1 green chile, finely chopped
salt to taste

FOR THE TAMARIND CHUTNEY
4oz tamarind, seeded, soaked in
   ⅓ cup water
2 tablespoons sugar
pinch of dried red chiles
pinch of salt
1 onion, finely chopped
a few mint leaves, chopped

makes 6 frankies

A favorite snack that Deepti loves to pick up during a long drive, this is usually sold in small kiosks along Mumbai's arterial roads. Once prepared, it is wrapped in a snug paper bag that is slipped down as you bite along the length. This recipe comes from a frankie seller and has been adapted for home cooking.

Mix the flour, oil, and a pinch of salt with about 5 tablespoons of water to make a smooth dough. Knead it for 2–3 minutes to get the right texture. Set aside for 30 minutes. Knead once more for 1 minute.

Divide the dough into six equal portions and roll each into a ball. Grease your hands with a little oil and flatten the balls into discs in the palm of your hand and then roll them out into thin rounds about 6–7 inches in diameter.

Heat a skillet on a low heat, add ½ teaspoon of oil and fry one side of a dough round for 1–2 minutes, then add another ½ teaspoon oil and fry the other side for another 1–2 minutes. Repeat with the other dough rounds and set aside.

To make the stuffing, mash the potatoes and mix in the onions, cilantro, green chile and salt to taste. Divide the mixture into six equal portions.

Next, make the tamarind chutney. Mash the tamarind into the soaking water with your hands and push the mixture through a strainer to remove the solids. Add the sugar and red chiles, together with a little salt, and then mix in the onion and mint leaves.

Finally, assemble the frankies: heat a clean skillet, add a little oil and reheat a frankie on both sides. Spread some egg mix on one side of the frankies, turn it over and cook for about 1 minute to cook the egg, then turn the frankie over egg-side up. Spread a portion of the potato stuffing in a line down the center. Add 1 tablespoon of tamarind chutney on top and fold over the two sides to make a roll. Drizzle a little extra tamarind chutney on top. Repeat with the remaining frankies.

Serve hot as a complete snack.

Bhariyal Karela

STUFFED BITTER GOURD

12 karelas or bitter gourds
3 tablespoons salt
5 tablespoons mustard oil

FOR THE STUFFING
2 tablespoons mustard oil
3 large onions, very finely chopped
2in piece of fresh ginger root, peeled
   and finely chopped
8 garlic cloves, finely sliced
1 tablespoon powdered cumin seeds
1 teaspoon turmeric
1 tablespoon powdered coriander seed
1 tablespoon red chili powder
1 tablespoon salt
1 green mango, skinned and chopped fine,
   or 1 tablespoon amchoor (mango
   powder)

serves 6

Karela, a bitter vegetable, is turned into this delicious dish through a process that removes its harsh edge. The final dish is unusual in flavor, tangy with a touch of spicy bitterness. Deepti loves the way her mother, Himadri Naval, used to make this and she shared the recipe with us from New York. You will need some thread to bind in the stuffing while cooking the karelas.

Scrape the crinkly, hard surface of the gourds with a knife until the skin is smooth and pale green. Don't discard the thin stem, as it comes in handy when working with the vegetable.

Slit the gourds in two along the length. If the karelas are old, there may be hard seeds inside that must be removed. If the inside pulp is tender, the seeds can be left in.

Salt the karelas all over and set aside for 20 minutes. Squeeze them to remove the bitter water, rinse under cold water and pat dry.

To make the stuffing, heat the oil in a skillet and just as it starts to smoke add the onions and sauté for 1 minute. Add the ginger, garlic, cumin, turmeric, and the coriander and red chili powders. Fry for 2 minutes, taking care not to let the spices stick to the pan. Add the salt and green mangoes or amchoor. Stir, remove from the heat and leave to cool.

Fill the open bellies of the karelas with the cooled stuffing (approximately 1 heaped tablespoon of filling per karela). Tie the thread all around the karela in a continuous loop to hold in the stuffing. There is no need to knot it, it will stay in place on its own.

In a skillet, heat the oil and gently add the stuffed karelas. Cook over a high heat until the skin is sealed, about 2 minutes. Add 4 tablespoons of water and, cover the pan. Cook for 3–4 minutes, then uncover and turn the karelas over, put the lid back on and cook for a further 3–4 minutes

Remove the thread, and serve with dal and hot rotis (see page 155).

Sabut Gobi Masala

WHOLE CAULIFLOWER MASALA

1 large cauliflower
3 tablespoons vegetable oil

FOR THE MASALA
4 onions, roughly chopped
4 garlic cloves
2in piece of fresh ginger root, peeled and
    roughly chopped
1 teaspoon red chili powder
2 whole green chiles, chopped
3 tablespoons mango powder (amchoor)
2 tablespoons ground coriander
a bunch of cilantro, roughly chopped
1 teaspoon turmeric
2 teaspoons garam masala (see page 154)
1 teaspoon salt

serves 6

"Masala" comes from Arabic and is used to describe Indian spice mixes, of which there are many. What makes this dish interesting is that the whole cauliflower is served in the center of the platter, with the raw salad items around it. In most Indian dishes, the cauliflower is broken into florets and they usually lose definition when served. Deepti Naval recalls this masala with nostalgia as a memorable dish made by her mother, who lived in Burma, Lahore, and Amritsar before moving to New York.

Preheat the oven to 350°F.

Whizz together the ingredients for the masala in a food-processor. The onions should give out enough liquid to make a smooth paste; if not, add 2 tablespoons of water.

Fry the masala in oil over a low heat for about 20 minutes until the oil leaves the sides of the masala and the onion changes color from pink to light brown. Remove from the heat and leave to cool for 15 minutes.

Wash the cauliflower gently and cut off the stem, leaving ½–1inch to keep the florets intact. Once the masala has cooled, stuff it into the grooves of the cauliflower.

Put the cauliflower in an oven dish just large enough to fit it and bake it in the oven for 40 minutes.

Remove from the oven and arrange the whole cauliflower in the center of a serving platter. Scallions, tomatoes, and green chiles can be used to decorate the cauliflower or served on the side.

This dish goes well with rotis or chappatis.

Rakesh Roshan, actor, director, and producer, was born into the film milieu. His father, known as Roshan, was a celebrated music composer in films and played the jal tarang (an instrument made up of china bowls filled with water, each struck with a light wooden mallet to make it ring). The family was often visited by many stylish actors, which inspired a young Rakesh to dream of acting. After his father's death when he was barely sixteen he went to work as an assistant director and a few years later Rajindra Kumar, the popular lead star of the 1960s and a family friend, provided him with his first acting opportunity. Starting with *Ghar Ghar Ki Kahani* in 1970, Rakesh went on to star in about sixty films. His passion for cinema has led him to write, produce, and direct many films, all marked with strong gripping drama and a good music score, often composed by his brother Rajesh Roshan.

The Roshans

Rakesh was a great mentor and role model to his son, Hrithik. Hrithik first achieved fame when he starred in *Kaho Na Pyaar Hai*, which was directed by his father and became the biggest blockbuster of 2000, earning him a best newcomer and best actor award. It was apparent that Hrithik was a major star in the making. However, the huge success of the film made Rakesh the target of organized crime gangs. He was shot by a member of the Mumbai underworld but miraculously survived and went on to direct another huge hit, *Koi Mil Gaya* (2003), again starring Hrithik.

Rakesh enjoyed a mixed and varied cuisine as he grew up, since his father came from Punjab and his mother from Bengal. He continues to enjoy all kinds of food; "I think the only thing I could resist were monkey's brains and snakes!" he chuckles. "I like cooking—it's a stress buster. I used to make really good meat and chicken curries, adding new flavors to familiar dishes. Friends liked my cooking, which was encouraging. Cooking for my kids was such a joy—making them mashed potatoes and mango milkshakes." Talking to Hrithik later about his most memorable meals he spontaneously says, "My dad's cooking was fabulous. His parathas, eggs, and curries especially. Now he has no time away from work," he adds wistfully.

Hrithik used to be a real fast-food junkie who loved McDonald's burgers (he could eat three or four!) and Subway sandwiches. But his quest for a sculpted body has made him more disciplined about food. Burgers and white bread have been replaced with rotis made with soya, nachni (finger millet), jowar, and bajra (Indian millets). He has a special diet combining Indian and Italian cuisines, and incorporates a strict exercise regime into his daily routine.

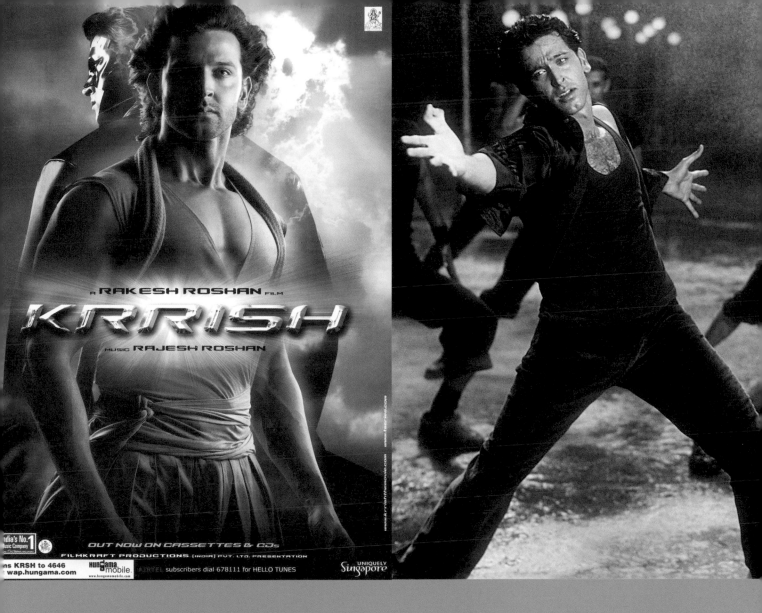

Both Rakesh and Hrithik love to eat out: in Mumbai they are frequent visitors of Wasabi at the Taj Mahal and the Thai Pavilion at Taj President. In London they love Nobu and in America they recommend P.F. Chang's which they describe as "the best, ultimate Chinese food in the world." And don't even try to keep them away from the New York Cheesecake Factory.

Interestingly, all of Rakesh's directorial works have titles starting with the letter 'K'. There is a little-known story behind it. "When I had made *Jaag Utha Insaan* and it did not do well at the box office, a fan called up and said I must use 'K' for all my film titles as it is lucky for me. Though I didn't believe it then, my first directorial film *Khudgarz* did really well and he called me again to remind me of his prediction. It has worked very well for me so far!" *Krrish* opened with record-breaking box office takings in 2006 and has been very popular with young people across India. Let's hope that the magic of 'K' continues for the Roshans!

above left: *Krrish* (2006) is the sequel to *Koi Mil Gaya* (2003) and the Roshan effect was once more in full swing—the film was a huge commercial hit. Hrithik plays a superhero with the help of great special effects.

above right: Hrithik's dancing has always been distinctive and highly appreciated and here he serenades Kareena Kapoor in *Yaadein* (2001).

Palak Paneer

SPINACH WITH FRESH COTTAGE CHEESE

TO MAKE FRESH PANEER
3½ pints full-fat milk
2 tablespoons lemon juice

TO MAKE PALAK PANEER
18oz spinach, washed and stems removed
1 tablespoon ghee (see page 155)
1 onion, chopped
1 tablespoon ginger paste (see page 155)
1 tablespoon garlic paste (see page 155)
2 tomatoes, skinned and chopped
1 tablespoon garam masala
    (see page 154)
1 tablespoon dried fenugreek leaves
2 green chiles, seeds removed and
    finely chopped
salt to taste
⅓ cup milk (optional)
14oz paneer, cut into 1¼in cubes

serves 4

Hrithik loves paneer in all forms. This recipe is extremely healthy as the spinach is full of iron and minerals and it is cooked with minimal oil. Paneer is condensed milk solids, available in India as blocks sold by weight. The best flavored paneer is fresh and soft, so below is a recipe to make it at home. Tofu can be used as an alternative to paneer. Traditionally, paneer is fried until the edges are lightly browned to give it a crunchy bite. To do this, fry the paneer in 4 tablespoons of ghee before adding it to the dish.

To make fresh paneer, bring the milk to a boil in a heavy saucepan and add the lemon juice. Remove from the heat and leave for 10 minutes for the milk to separate into whey and curds.

Line a colander with cheesecloth or muslin and drain the whey. Carefully tie up the cheesecloth and place a heavy weight on top to help drain the remaining liquid. You can also hang it in a cheesecloth to let gravity work the water out, this will take about 30 minutes. When all whey has left the solids, the paneer can be refrigerated until needed. This recipe should yield 12–14 ounces paneer, depending on the quality of the milk you use.

To make Palak Paneer, roughly chop the spinach and steam-cook it for 5 minutes. Leave to cool for 15 minutes, then place in a food-processor and blend for 30 seconds on the minimum setting.

Heat the ghee in a saucepan and sauté the onion until light brown. Add the ginger and garlic pastes and sauté for 1 minute. Stir in the tomatoes, garam masala, and fenugreek and continue to cook for 2 minutes stirring continuously. Add the green chiles and continue cooking and stirring for 1 minute.

Add the spinach paste and a little salt and cook for 3 minutes on a low heat. You can add some milk at this stage for a creamier version of the dish. When the milk is thoroughly hot, add the cubes of paneer and remove from the heat.

Serve hot, with rotis or boiled rice.

Phirni

½ cup basmati rice
2½ pints full-fat milk
1⅔ cup sugar
½ teaspoon saffron strands, soaked in
　3 tablespoons cold milk
seeds of 5 cardamoms, ground (with husks)
10 almonds, blanched and sliced
10 pistachios, sliced

serves 6

Phirni is a favorite dessert of Hrithik's. It is originally from Kashmir and is served set in earthen pots that are often decorated with Indian lace. Fragrant, lightly sweet and creamy in texture, this is a mouth-watering dessert served at celebratory events and is available in most Muslim restaurants of Mumbai.

Wash the rice and soak it in water (the water level should reach 1¼ inches above the rice) for 1 hour.

Set aside ⅓ cup of the milk. Bring the remainder to a boil, then simmer on a low heat for 20 minutes so that it reduces and thickens. Stir in the sugar until it dissolves.

Meanwhile, grind the soaked rice in a blender for 1 minute. Add the ⅓ cup of cold milk and stir until smooth.

Stir the rice mixture into the thickened milk and cook for 15 minutes, stirring continuously to prevent the rice sticking to the bottom of the pan and burning.

Add the saffron-infused milk, ground cardamom, sliced almonds, and pistachios, then let cool. Refrigerate until needed.

Serve chilled, preferably in individual earthenware pots.

Tall, graceful, and a wonderful dancer, Shilpa is the typical glamorous actress that Bollywood idolizes. She has a perfect hourglass figure that she insists is "genetically engineered" since both her parents were models in their youth. Shilpa began her career modeling but started acting when she was cast in the film *Baazigar* (1993), a mega hit starring Shah Rukh Khan and Kajol. However, things could have been very different for Shilpa. "I thought I would be a volleyball coach some day. Films were never something I had planned on doing."

Shilpa Shetty

Now, after ten years as an actress, she has a huge fan base who admire her energetic dance routines and song sequences, some of which have even outlived the films. Recently, her sensitive performance in *Phir Milenge* (2004), where she plays a woman with HIV, earned her several awards and recognition as a serious actress. Shilpa also supports the PETA animal welfare cause and is keen to use her fame to help create awareness of these issues.

Shilpa enjoys a wide range of food. She is a big fan of sushi and will go all the way into downtown Mumbai to Wasabi, a Japanese restaurant at Taj Mahal. She also loves Chinese food—Royal China in London is top of her list. "Now they have come to Mumbai, that's so great" she says joyfully. "Chinese food is so healthy, the vegetables are lightly cooked and it matches my high protein low carb regimen."

Shilpa also loves to cook. "I joined weekend cooking classes when I was 13 or 14 years old and my teacher, Charu Mehta, was a Gujarati lady who taught us many different techniques and dishes. She was really talented and we loved getting the opportunity to taste her dishes. Later I began experimenting with soups, adding a new ingredient every time I cooked. Now I realize that cooking is all about love and creativity. I make great corn pulao. I have even served it to Salman Khan." In the course of her experiments, she has evolved a pink sauce, a mix of arrabiata and white sauce in which she adds chicken, sausages, mushrooms, and zucchini with basil. She promises it is fantastic.

She was raised on traditional Mangalorean dishes, and she still loves cari roti and mackerel pickle. Since the use of coconuts is central to this cuisine, her mother would replace the rich coconut with skimmed milk to keep everyone healthy. Her grandmother was an amazing cook and Shilpa remembers her fondly. "I lived with her at one point and remember even her simple steamed green beans with grated coconut and chili were divine. I really miss her cooking. As kids my cousins and I would have to be on good behavior if we wanted our favorite soup and we would queue up for it—alphabets floating in clear consommé." Another strong memory is of the gooey chocolate cake made by one of her aunts that she only got to eat on vacations and would taste different every time. "I find it strange that food can turn out so differently even when made meticulously with the same recipe," she says wonderingly. Shilpa is excited about the dynamic nature of cooking and looks forward to discovering new recipes as much as new roles in her forthcoming films.

SPICY FINE BEANS

2 tablespoons vegetable oil
pinch of asafoetida
1 teaspoon black mustard seeds
2 tablespoons split skinned black lentils
 (urad dal)
5 curry leaves
1 onion, chopped
18oz fine beans, topped, tailed,
 and halved
5 green chiles, seeded and
 chopped into rings
1 teaspoon sugar
salt to taste

serves 6

This is one of Shilpa's own recipes and she loves the crunchy flavors.

Heat the oil in a pan. Add the asafoetida, mustard seeds, urad dal, and curry leaves. Stir-fry till the dal turns reddish.

Add the onion, beans, and green chiles and stir-fry for a couple of minutes. Add a little salt and the sugar and 1 cup of water, cover the pan and simmer gently for about 10 minutes. (Shilpa's mother has a clever tip to know when the dish is done. She puts a cup of water on the saucepan lid and waits until the water evaporates.)

Serve hot, with fish curry and rice.

Cori Roti

MANGALOREAN-STYLE CHICKEN CURRY

2lbs chicken
2 tablespoons vegetable oil
1 teaspoon fenugreek seeds
1 teaspoon mustard seeds
8–9 curry leaves
2 onions, finely chopped
2 tomatoes, skinned and chopped
1 tablespoon ginger-garlic paste
   (see page 155)
3 green chiles, slit lengthways
1 teaspoon red chili powder

½ teaspoon cumin seeds
1 teaspoon ground coriander
½ teaspoon turmeric
1 teaspoon freshly ground black pepper
1¼oz seedless tamarind, soaked in
   3½ tablespoons water for 20 minutes and
   strained
2oz jaggery, soaked in 3½ tablespoons water for
   20 minutes and strained
3 cups 2% milk
a handful of cilantro leaves, chopped
salt to taste

serves 6

This is a family favorite. Shilpa's mother, Sunanda Shetty, has modified the classic version to make it low in cholesterol; the original uses coconut milk.

Cut the chicken into eight pieces, halving both the breasts and leg pieces. Put it into a large saucepan with 2 cups of water, bring to a gentle boil and cook for 30 minutes. Alternatively, roast the chicken in a medium oven, preheated to 350°F, for 50 minutes or so, until the chicken is fully cooked.

In a separate large saucepan, heat the oil and add the fenugreek and mustard seeds and the curry leaves and let them splutter for 30 seconds. Then add the onions and stir constantly, taking care not to let the spices burn, until golden brown.

Add the tomatoes, ginger-garlic paste, and the chiles and sauté for about 3–5 minutes until smooth. Add the cooked chicken and the dry spices—red chili powder, cumin seeds, ground coriander, turmeric, and black pepper—and stir over a low heat. Add some salt, the tamarind and the soaked jaggery and its water and bring to a boil. Finally add the milk and boil for a further 5 minutes. Garnish with chopped cilantro and serve hot.

This aromatic curry is usually eaten with a hard roti available at Karnataka stores. The curry is poured over both sides of the roti and allowed to soak for a few minutes to soften it, then both roti and curry are eaten together. It can also be eaten with tandoori roti, rice, or any hard bread.

Sukha Lamb

DRY LAMB MANGALOREAN STYLE

2lbs lamb or mutton, preferably from
   the leg and cut into 2in pieces
salt and freshly ground black pepper
3 tablespoons vegetable oil
1 teaspoon fenugreek seeds
1 teaspoon black mustard seeds
8–9 curry leaves
2 onions, finely chopped
1 tablespoon ginger-garlic paste
   (see page 155)
2 tomatoes, skinned and chopped
3 green chiles, slit lengthways
2 tablespoons red chili powder
1 tablespoon ground coriander
1 tablespoon cumin seeds
1 tablespoon turmeric
1 tablespoon freshly ground black pepper
1 coconut, shredded to a coarse paste
   (by running through a food-processor
   for 30 seconds)
a handful of cilantro leaves, chopped

serves 6

This recipe also comes from Sunanda Shetty. She often uses mutton in this dish but lamb is good too. Sunanda also uses this method to cook chicken but Shilpa prefers it with mutton.

Season the lamb with a little salt and black pepper and place it in a large saucepan. Pour in ⅓ cup of water to just cover the meat. Bring to simmering point, cover the pan and cook for about 45 minutes until the lamb is just tender.

In a large wide saucepan, heat the oil and fry the fenugreek seeds, mustard seeds, and curry leaves. Once they darken (1–2 minutes), add the onions and ginger-garlic paste and stir-fry until golden brown.

Add the tomatoes and green chiles and the red chili powder, ground coriander, cumin seeds, turmeric, and black pepper. Season with salt and keep stirring until mixture is smooth.

Add the cooked lamb or mutton together with its cooking liquid and stir in the shredded coconut. Keep cooking over a low heat for 10 minutes until all the liquid evaporates and the flavors have seeped through the meat. Garnish with cilantro leaves and serve hot, with rice and a vegetable and tomato saar.

right: Shilpa Shetty is a great dancer and she can draw audiences in droves with her moves. This picture is taken from a gypsy dance sequence in a village setting for *Badhai Ho Badhai* (2002).

Tomato Saar

MANGALOREAN TOMATO CURRY

2 tablespoons vegetable oil
2 onions, finely chopped
6 large tomatoes, skinned and
    chopped fine
5 green chiles, cut lengthways
1 cinnamon stick
2 carrots, finely chopped
4oz fine beans, finely
    chopped
1 teaspoon sugar
salt to taste

FOR THE TEMPERING
1 tablespoon vegetable oil
pinch of asafoetida
½ teaspoon turmeric
1 teaspoon black mustard seeds
5–6 curry leaves

FOR THE GARNISH
a handful of cilantro leaves,
    chopped

serves 6

Heat the oil in a large saucepan and add the onions, cooking until just softened. Add the tomatoes, green chiles, carrots, fine beans and sugar together with 1¾ cups of water and simmer for 15 minutes in the uncovered pan.

Heat the oil in a small skillet and add the asafoetida, tumeric, black mustard seeds, and curry leaves. As they splutter and darken, pour them into the tomato curry. Garnish with cilantro leaves.

This tomato curry is eaten with rice, meat, and fish dishes in a Mangalorean meal.

MANGALOREAN-STYLE FISH CURRY

3 tablespoons vegetable oil
pinch of asafoetida
1 tablespoon fenugreek seeds
1 teaspoon cumin seeds
6 curry leaves
2 onions, shredded
2 tablespoons ginger-garlic
    paste (see page 155)
5 green chiles, cut
    lengthways
2 teaspoons ground
    coriander
1 teaspoon turmeric

1 teaspoon freshly ground
    black pepper
1 tablespoon tamarind paste
5 kokum soaked in a little
    water (optional)
    (see page 142)
6 pomfret fillets (or any flat
    white fish)
1 cup milk
1 teaspoon sugar
a large handful of cilantro
    leaves, chopped
salt to taste

serves 6

In a wide saucepan, heat the oil and add the asafoetida, fenugreek seeds, cumin seeds, and curry leaves. As they darken add the onions and ginger-garlic paste and stir for a few minutes. Add the green chiles, ground coriander, turmeric, and black pepper. Reduce the heat and add the tamarind paste and kokum.

Place the fish fillets in the pan. Cook on a low heat for 2 minutes and then turn over. Add the milk, sugar, and salt and cook gently for a further 5 minutes.

Garnish with cilantro and serve hot, with boiled rice.

From the time he was born, Suneil Shetty has been surrounded by food. His community (Mangalorean Bunts) own and run ninety percent of the fast-food restaurants in Maharashtra. His father, Veerappa Shetty, came to Mumbai when he was nine years old and worked his way from a trainee to owning the very restaurants he worked in. "Food has always been a matter of pride for me" Suneil claims. He worked in his father's restaurants during school vacations and through college. "I was a master at managing the kitchen and the bar, the stocktaking, the layout of kitchen. My fascination is with the business side of food." He now owns the Mischief restaurant at the Opera House and a more recent venture, Salt Water Grill, an open-air restaurant on the Chowpatty Beach at Marine Drive.

Suneil Shetty

Suneil's taste buds are simple, with a penchant for home cooking. He likes to eat his breakfast like a king, lunch like a prince and dinner like a pauper. Food from Mangalore especially fascinates him—the temple food in particular. Rasam, rice, pooris, melons, pickles, chutneys, papads, all served on banana leaves. "My mom is the best cook in the world and even her food tastes better in Mangalore. It's the flavors of the local ingredients. Especially the coconut, that is so sweet there and is used in a lot of our food."

Suneil was interested in martial arts from a young age and he trained in a traditional form of karate, before learning full contact kickboxing. This training has taught him grace, style, and elegant body movements. He was introduced to cinema through the director-producers Rajiv Rai and J P Dutta. He initially got roles for his martial arts skills, "acting I learnt on the way," he says candidly. He has recently begun to take on more comic roles that he is enjoying enormously.

Essentially a family man, Suneil loves to go home when work wraps up and be with his children—playing football with his son Ahan or reading with his daughter, Athya. He loves getting away to Mangalore as much as possible, living on the farm amidst the sounds of roosters, cows, and gurgling water. Even after seventeen years in films, he often forgets he is an actor and has caught himself wondering why people are staring at him. His down-to-earth nature has earned him tremendous goodwill and respect in the film industry, where he is often refered to as "Anna" (elder brother).

Suneil has traveled extensively and believes that hospitality is vital to a good meal. He has been very impressed with Balinese cuisine, where the food and ambience struck a chord with him. He has also found the Pakistani *khatirdari* (hospitality) warm and endearing. "I felt like a son-in-law getting the red carpet treatment."

Kori Sukka

SPICY DRY CHICKEN

3 tablespoons ghee (see page 155)
    or butter
3 tablespoons coriander seeds
¾ teaspoon turmeric
1½ teaspoons black peppercorns
¾ teaspoon fennel seeds
1½ teaspoons fenugreek seeds
1½ teaspoons poppy seeds
18 whole dried red chiles, roasted
    (dry-roast for about 3 minutes on
    a griddle)
1 tablespoon tamarind paste
1 coconut, shredded
3–4 garlic cloves
1½ teaspoons cumin seeds
3lbs chicken, skinless, cut into
    about 12 pieces
8 curry leaves
1½ large onions, finely chopped
salt to taste

serves 6

This dish comes from the Bunt community, Hindis from Mangalore in South India. Their cuisine, now very popular in Mumbai, is notable for "badige" (a type of red chile available locally) and coconut. The gravy is usually a mix of dry spices in coconut milk called "gassi." This recipe comes from Suneil's kitchen and he takes great pride in its presentation.

Heat ½ tablespoon ghee or butter and roast the coriander seeds, turmeric, black peppercorns and the fennel, fenugreek and poppy seeds. Once the aroma starts to rise, take the saucepan off the heat and leave to cool. Add the whole red chiles and tamarind paste and grind to a paste. Set aside.

Coarsely grind tgether the shredded coconut, garlic, and cumin seeds without adding any water. This should take 1–2 whizzes in a food-processor. This coconut paste should be coarse and dry.

Mix the chicken with the first paste and leave to rest for 10 minutes. In a large skillet with a lid, heat 1½ tablespoons of the ghee or butter over a low heat, add the chicken and stir to coat it well. Cook gently, covered, for 30 minutes (without adding any water). Open and stir occasionally. The chicken will be almost done by now.

Add the coconut paste and a pinch of salt. Cover and cook for a further 5 minutes or until the chicken is cooked.

In a small skillet heat the remaining ghee or butter, add the curry leaves and fry for 1 minute. Add the onions and continue to fry until they are light brown. Pour this as a garnish over the chicken and serve hot.

This dish goes well with ghee rice (plain white rice with fresh ghee poured on top—an acquired taste for those not used to South Indian cuisine), plain boiled rice, or roti.

Uppittu

This Mangalorean snack is often eaten at breakfast or with late-afternoon coffee.

Heat a heavy saucepan and dry-roast the semolina until it very slightly changes color. Set aside and allow to cool.

First make the tempering. Heat the oil in a saucepan and add the peanuts, mustard seeds, urad dal, chiles and curry leaves. Once the mustard seeds are spluttering, add the asafoetida and turmeric and cook for 1 minute, stirring to make sure the spices don't stick to the base of the pan.

Add the onions and, when they are translucent, stir in the potato slices and coat them well in the tempering ingredients. Pour in 1 cup of water and some salt and let the potatoes cook until tender.

Reduce the heat and add the ginger and sugar. Finally add the roasted semolina, little by little, stirring continuously to avoid forming lumps.

Cover with a lid and cook for a few minutes.

Garnish with chopped cilantro and shredded coconut. Pour the ghee over the top and serve hot.

7oz semolina
1 onion, sliced
1 potato, sliced
1in piece of fresh ginger root, peeled and shredded
1 tablespoon granulated sugar
a small bunch of cilantro, chopped (about 2oz)
4 tablespoons shredded fresh coconut
3 tablespoons ghee (see page 155)
salt to taste

FOR THE TEMPERING
4 tablespoons vegetable oil
3 tablespoons peanuts
2 teaspoons black mustard seeds
2 teaspoons split skinned black lentils (urad dal)
3 whole dried red chiles
5–6 curry leaves
pinch of asafoetida
½ teaspoon turmeric

serves 6

Marvai Ajhadhina

SHELLFISH IN MANGALOREAN MASALA

30 medium-sized clams
1 coconut, shredded
2 tablespoons cumin seeds
2 garlic cloves, cut into tiny flakes
3 tablespoons coconut oil
30 whole red chiles
2 tablespoons coriander seeds
½ tablespoon fenugreek seeds
1 tablespoon black peppercorns
½ teaspoon turmeric
3 onions, chopped
2 tablespoons tamarind paste
    (1½–2oz tamarind soaked in
    3½ tablespoons water and strained)
salt to taste

serves 6

This dry preparation is mouth-watering and fiery hot! Do reduce the chili to suit your tastes. This dish is addictive and may be eaten as an appetizer or a main course; either way, it goes well with beer. Use quahog or littleneck clams if you can get them.

Wash the shellfish thoroughly to remove any mud and sand. When completely clean break open the shells and keep the fleshy side, discarding the other. They must not be washed after breaking the shells.

Make a coarse paste with the coconut, half the cumin seeds, and a third of the garlic flakes.

In two tablespoons of coconut oil, fry the red chiles, coriander seeds, remaining cumin seeds, the fenugreek seeds, black peppercorns, turmeric powder, a third of the garlic flakes, and two-thirds of the onions. Once the onions are lightly browned, remove from the heat and leave to cool. Then grind to a paste, adding 1 tablespoon of water if needed.

In a large saucepan, add the paste to the cleaned shellfish and cover. Cook on a low heat and, after 3–4 minutes, add the coconut paste and tamarind. Cook for a further 3–4 minutes. In a skillet, heat the remaining coconut oil and fry the remaining onion and garlic until deep brown. Mix into the shellfish and serve hot, with dosas.

Kane Ghashi/Nogli

MANGALOREAN LADYFISH CURRY

1¾lbs ladyfish, (or other firm white fish)
   cleaned and cut into 6 slices
2 tablespoons coconut oil
1 onion, finely chopped
salt to taste

FOR THE PASTE
1 coconut, shredded (or use coconut milk)
8 whole dried red chiles, roasted in
   1 tablespoon coconut oil
1 tablespoon tamarind paste

serves 6

To be Mangalorean is to love nogli/kane (ladyfish). Ladyfish is available along the western coast of India but it can be replaced with any lean, firm, white fish. This curry is very spicy, so if you prefer milder dishes reduce the red chiles to half or less and remove the seeds. Coconut oil is particular to Mangalorean cuisine and must be tried at least once. If the taste cannot be acquired, you can use vegetable oil instead.

First make the paste by grinding together the coconut, chiles, and tamarind paste to a smooth texture.

Put the fish slices in a heavy saucepan and gently stir in the paste so that the fish is well covered. Sprinkle with a little salt. Add about ¾ cup of water and bring to a boil, then reduce the heat, cover and simmer for 10 minutes. The curry will be thick, its consistency can be adjusted by adding more water—since it is very spicy, you may prefer a thinner curry. Make sure that the fish is not overcooked as it tends to disintegrate.

In a small skillet, heat the coconut oil and fry the onions untill they are medium-brown.

Pour the onions over the curry. Cover and swirl the pan to mix in the onions. Avoid using spoons or other utensils as the fish is delicate. The art of making this dish is to keep the fish in chunky pieces.

Serve hot, with boiled rice.

opposite page: When Jackie Shroff met his mentor Subhash Ghai he asked to be cast as a villain in a film. In a complete role reversal the director cast him as his lead in a film called *Hero* (1983).

In south Mumbai the last of the Iranian restaurants, with their quaint character and simple yet definitive menus, still abound. As a young boy, Jackie Shroff loved having breakfast there with his father. They would devour brun maska (hard bread roll with butter) with sugar dipped into pani-kam-chai (milky tea) to the crackle of newspaper sheets being turned and the sizzle of eggs being cooked. On the counter would be a display of pastries, gooey with heavy icing, that he recalls left an aftertaste tingle on the tongue.

In the town of Teen Batti in Mumbai, where Jackie grew up in a one-room home, there were many food delights. Down the street was a little Indian restaurant where the poori bhaji (puffed fried roti with thick vegetable masala stew), yellow sheera (dessert made with semolina), and badam halwa (almond and flour dessert) were scrumptious. At Hanging Gardens, the seekh kabobs were inviting when freshly grilled on open hot coals served with thin mint chutney. As a teenager his usual hangout was an Iranian restaurant called New York. "Crocodile Rock on the jukebox and beer with French fries. That was living it up!" Jackie had a gang of friends who were forever getting into trouble and he would always bail them out. He earned the sobriquet "Jaggu Dada" (dada is an elder who protects) and it stuck with him during his film years, when it was often his screen name too.

Jackie Shroff

Jackie loves to cook and his first teacher was his nose. Too small to see his mother cook, he would trail behind her and follow the journey through the aromas. A few years later, tall enough to watch, he began to understand the nuances of food. Jackie believes that contact between metal and raw food should be minimal. "Food needs gentleness. Use your hands as much as possible, not the knife. Pluck the leaves tenderly; it will make a difference to the taste." He has been studying the way food can benefit the body and believes that fruit eaten at the end of a meal can be toxic and that soups should be consumed at the end of a meal rather than at the beginning. "Have your pineapples and watermelons before other foods to avoid the bloated feeling they give," he advises. Another interesting concept he shared is the relationship between water and food. Those who have water with food are bhogi (ruled by the senses), those who have water after food are rogi (ruled by illness), and those who have water before meals are yogi (ruled by perfect health).

Jackie is a diverse actor who brings energy and depth to the characters he plays. His film career took off in the 1980s with the hit film *Hero*, Subhash Ghai's first film, and since then he has acted in an astonishing 180 films— and he looks good enough for another 180!

It is not a "Love Story"
It is a "Lovely" Story!

SUNEHA ARTS

PREM DEEWANE

IT'S A **MUKTA ARTS**
PRESENTATION

PRODUCED BY
ASHOK GHAI
DIRECTED BY
SACHIN

Bhuna Baingan

ROAST EGGPLANT

4 large eggplant
20 garlic cloves
8 whole green chiles
4 tablespoons mustard oil or sesame oil
  (cold-pressed is best)
salt to taste

serves 6

Jackie is quite particular about ingredients and for most of his dishes he uses cold pressed oils rather than the refined oils available in the supermarket. He also advocates the use of tea oil and organic foods.

Take the eggplant and insert 5 garlic cloves and 2 green chiles into each of them so that they look almost like porcupines.

Traditionally, the eggplant is cooked in the hot ashes of a tandoor oven for 10 minutes. In the absence of a tandoor, you can get a similar effect by holding them over a gas flame. Once the peel is blackened and cracking, gently remove the char and mash the flesh of the eggplant with the garlic and the green chiles.

Season with salt and pour the oil on top. Mix and serve.

These are great eaten with tandoori roti.

Methi Aaloo

POTATOES IN FENUGREEK LEAVES

large bunch of fresh fenugreek leaves
3 tablespoons groundnut oil,
   cold-pressed
6 large potatoes, peeled and diced
4 garlic cloves
3 large, ripe tomatoes, skinned
   and puréed
salt to taste

serves 6

This dish is Jackie's favorite, and is utterly simple to prepare.

Gently remove the fenugreek leaves from the stem (they should never be chopped as Jackie believes this ruins the flavor).

Heat the oil in a skillet and add the diced potato. Once it starts to color, add the garlic. Continue to cook until the potato is browned on all sides.

Keeping the heat low, sprinkle the fenugreek leaves over the potatoes. Make a shallow well in the center and spoon in the tomato purée. Cover the pan and steam-cook for 10 minutes. Turn once with a ladle to bring the potatoes to the top, then cover and cook for a further 10 minutes. Season with the salt and stir gently.

Serve hot with bajra, jawar, or plain rotis.

Pao Bhaji

BOMBAY-STYLE BREAD WITH SPICY POTATOES

18oz butter
2oz cumin seeds
4oz ginger-garlic paste (see page 155)
6 medium potatoes, boiled
6 medium tomatoes, skinned and chopped
2¾ cups green peas, boiled
4oz pao bhaji masala (see page 154)
4 tablespoons lime juice
large bunch cilantro leaves, chopped (about 4oz)
24 loaves of pao
3 medium onions, finely chopped
2 lemons, cut into wedges
salt to taste

serves 6

Jackie loves street-food and this classic dish, born right off the streets of Mumbai, is one of his favorite midnight snacks after a long shoot. Traditionally, this is cooked on a large, round, hot griddle while you watch; the paos are split in half and toasted in the butter and masala. Pao Bhaji Masala has become a proprietary blend and is widely available in Indian stores.

Heat half the butter in a large, heavy saucepan and add the cumin seeds and the ginger-garlic paste. Sauté lightly.

Add the potatoes, tomatoes, green peas and the pao bhaji masala. Mash the vegetables as they cook and let them soak in the spice mix and butter. Usually no salt is needed but taste and adjust to your palate. Remove from the heat, add the lime juice and stir.

Garnish with cilantro leaves and dollops of butter. Serve with fresh paos (4 per person), garnished with chopped onions and lemon wedges.

With a remarkable bone structure that gives her a distinct glamor, Raveena Tandon has gone from being the popular lead actress in mainstream films to working as a serious actress in art house films. It has been an exciting journey for her and one that she has enjoyed enormously. She has always had a distinctive onscreen presence and she manages to bridge the gap between Western and Indian styling with ease. Films such as *Mohra* (1994) were hugely popular and turned her into the defining spirit of the 1990s.

Raveena grew up in a Punjabi family where food was an important focus. Early morning kick-starts were paranthas in white butter and toasts with malai (natural milk cream) and sugar. Her love of Bengali sweets and gulab jamuns as a child earned her the nickname "full laddoo" (a big round sweet ball) in her family. Her father would threaten to marry her off to a halwai (a sweet maker). Her love of South Indian food started with the frequent family journeys to the shrine of Shirdi in Maharashtra. On the way to Shirdi, they would always stop at a restaurant called Dasaprakash and gorge on idlis and dosas. She savored the coconut chutney served with both these dishes more than anything else.

Raveena Tandon

Today, she is very aware that she needs to be more careful about what she eats, but doesn't believe in having too limited a diet or restricting herrself. She combines her favorite coconut chutney with healthier foods such as steamed fish, soup, salads, and sprouts with chaat-style masalas. Raveena also believes in the ayurvedic principle of eating a small amount of pure ghee every day for good health. She substitutes sugar with dates and raisins, and even her daughter's first solid foods were sweetened by these natural sources. She prefers organic vegetables and gets unpolished rice and mangoes from her farm to guarantee her family's health and well-being.

With the birth of her baby girl, Raveena decided to take a sabbatical from acting. This gave her the opportunity to be able to enjoy motherhood more fully and spend precious time with her family. It has also meant that she now has more time for cooking and has discovered a talent for experimenting with flavors and dishes. She is particularly good with European styles and loves making wholewheat pastas, risottos, and chicken and clam chowders. Her food is as diverse as the film roles she takes on, and Bollywood waits for her return with eagerness.

Sai Bhaji

SPINACH IN GRAM DAL

4oz gram dal, (channa dal) soaked
  in cold water for 20 minutes
2in piece of fresh ginger root, peeled
  and sliced
4 garlic cloves, peeled
4 large tomatoes, quartered
1 potato, peeled and quartered
3 green chiles, sliced in half
  lengthways
1 teaspoon turmeric
3 bunches of spinach, roughly
  chopped
salt to taste

serves 6

This Sindhi dish is vegetarian, low in calories and full of vibrant flavors.

Take a large saucepan with a tight-fitting lid and put in all the ingredients except the spinach, add ⅔ cup of water and cover. Bring to a boil over a high heat, discard any froth then reduce the heat and simmer gently for 40–50 minutes until the gram dal is almost tender. Add the spinach and cook for a further 2–3 minutes with the pan uncovered to preserve the color of the spinach, stirring frequently.

Mash the vegetables and dal using a madhaani (wooden hand-churner) or potato ricer. A blender is usually avoided as it makes the dal too smooth. The finished dish should have a leafy bite to it.

Serve hot, with boiled rice and a dry vegetable dish.

Khatti Dal

TANGY DAL

1½ cups yellow lentils (toor dal)
1 teaspoon turmeric
1½in piece of fresh ginger root,
  peeled and finely diced
3 tomatoes, chopped
2 green chiles, slit in half
  lengthways
2 tablespoons vegetable oil
2 tablespoons whole fenugreek seeds
⅓oz kokum (see page 142),
  soaked in water
salt to taste

serves 6

Raveena swears by her cook's ability to make this dal, that is a real favorite.

Put the dal in a heavy saucepan and add the turmeric, ginger, tomatoes, green chiles, and some salt. Pour over 2½ pints of water and bring to a boil. Discard any froth, reduce the heat and simmer gently for about 50 minutes.

Strain the dal to remove the tomato skins and ginger pieces and return it to the pan. The dal will be cooked and thin in consistency.

Heat the oil in a small skillet. Add the fenugreek seeds and, when they start to darken, add them to the dal.

Mash the kokum into the water and strain it. Add the drained water into the dal and bring to a boil, then remove from the heat.

Serve hot, with boiled rice and vegetables.

Sindhi Kadi

¾ cup yellow lentils (toor dal), soaked in cold water for 40 minutes

½ teaspoon turmeric

4 tomatoes, halved

5 tablespoons vegetable oil

a few curry leaves

1 tablespoon cumin seeds

½ tablespoon fenugreek seeds

½ teaspoon asafoetida powder

5 green chiles, slit in half lengthways

5 tablespoons gram flour

2½ teaspoons red chili powder

5oz okra, slit lengthways

4oz fine beans, stringed, topped, and tailed

1 lotus stem, cut into 1¼in pieces

4 potatoes, peeled and halved

6–7 kokum, soaked in 1½ tablespoons water

salt to taste

serves 6

Another classic from Raveena's Sindhi kitchen.

Put the dal into a large saucepan with the turmeric, tomatoes, and some salt and cover with 2½ cups of water. Bring to a boil, then simmer until the lentils are soft. Leave to cool slightly then stir well to blend to a soup-like consistency.

In another large saucepan, heat the oil and add the curry leaves, cumin seeds, fenugreek seeds, asafoetida powder, and green chiles. Fry for 2 minutes and add the gram flour, stirring all the time. Add the red chili powder and continue to stir for a few minutes until the gram flour turns light brown.

Tip the warm dal soup into the gram flour mix and stir constantly until thoroughly mixed. Then add the okra, fine beans, lotus stem, and potatoes and cook for 30–45 minutes, until the vegetables are just tender; they will absorb flavor from the spices.

Serve hot with basmati rice, potato cutlets, and sweet boondi.

Kokum is a dark purple flower that grows in central India and is mainly cultivated in Goa. It is used extensively in Goan and Mangalorean cooking both as a souring agent and for making sherbets because of its cooling properties. Kokum can be bought in specialty Indian stores as a dried rind or fruit; it colors everything it comes into contact with, so if you want to preserve the color of the dish, use lemon juice instead.

Dal Gosht

MUTTON IN GRAM LENTILS

4oz pure ghee (see page 155)
6 large onions thinly sliced
10 green cardamoms
1 teaspoon ground black
   cardamom pods
10 cloves
1 teaspoon turmeric
3 tablespoons ground coriander
2lbs mutton or lamb, cut into
   2in cubes

1 teaspoon ginger paste
   (see page 155)
1 teaspoon garlic paste
   (see page 155)
2 teaspoons red chili powder
7oz gram dal (channa dal),
   soaked for 1 hour in cold water
¾ cup plain yogurt
1 tablespoon salt
2 tablespoons cilantro
   leaves, chopped

serves 6

In a large saucepan, heat half the ghee and fry the onions until they are light brown. Cool and grind to a paste, adding a spoonful of water if needed, and set aside.

In the same pan heat the remaining ghee on a low heat and fry the green and black cardamoms, cloves, turmeric, and ground coriander until their flavors are released, (about 1–2 minutes) stirring constantly to avoid them sticking to the pan. Add the meat and onion paste and fry it with all the spices until the juices are sealed and the mutton turns light pink.

Add the ginger and garlic pastes and the red chili powder and stir for 1 minute. Mix in the gram dal and the yogurt, season with salt to taste and pour in enough water to just cover the mixture in the pan. Cover with a lid and simmer for about 1 hour. Stir the ingredients every few minutes to prevent the mixture sticking on the bottom, and ensure the heat is low throughout the cooking to bring out all the flavors.

When ready, the liquid will have mostly evaporated, leaving a deliciously thick curry of spiced dal and mutton. Garnish with fresh cilantro leaves.

Serve hot, with rice or rotis.

Gulab Jamun

250g sugar
2 tablespoons rose water
175g plain flour
50g powdered milk
150ml milk
250ml vegetable oil for frying
15–20 pistachios,
   roughly chopped

serves 6

Raveena is an expert at making these sweets and rattled off the recipe effortlessly.

First make your syrup: bring 1 litre of water to the boil in a heavy-based pan and add the sugar, stirring constantly until it dissolves. Boil until the syrup evaporates to one third of its original quantity. Allow to cool and then stir in the rose water and mix well.

In a bowl mix the flour and powdered milk and stir in the milk to make an elastic dough. Knead it until smooth on a lightly floured surface. Roll into small balls, about 3cm in diameter. These harden quite quickly so be ready to cook them immediately.

Heat the oil in a frying pan. Reduce the heat and add the balls one by one. Do not cook more than 4 at a time, and keep moving them with a ladle so that they get evenly browned. When they start to turn dark brown remove them with a slotted spoon. Cook the remaining balls in the same way.

Add the gulab jamuns to the syrup and let them soak for 15 minutes.

Serve garnished with the chopped pistachios.

Preity Zinta is clearly an outdoor girl who enjoys the thrill of adventure. "I like the notion of being on the edge and pulling back." Her previous holidays have included bungee jumping, sky-diving, and para-sailing. She trained as a gymnast from the age of four and played basketball in school and college.

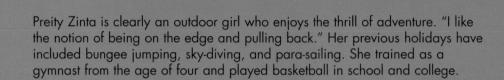

She went on to train as a criminal psychologist before Shekhar Kapur noticed her in an advert for lime soap and approached her to be in his film. *Tara Rum Pum Pum*, the film he cast her in, did not get made in the end but she had been noticed within the industry. Her debut release ended up being *Dil Se* (1998), where she starred opposite Shah Rukh Khan. After that success her future was assured and she embarked upon a roller coaster of film hits.

Her impish charm, effervescent personality and mischievous spirit have made her incredibly popular. She is looking forward to her new film *Kabhie Alvida Na Kehna*, which she thinks is the hardest role she has ever played, a real challenge. 'I play someone so contrary to myself that it was tough and also very enriching.'

Preity samples a lot of food in Mumbai and eating out is a frequent occurance. At Olive, chef Evan rustles up special dishes for her. She also loves Masala Bay and Ming Yang at Taj Land's End. She craves street food favourites like vada pao, pao bhaji and juices. When these are available in hygienic environs, Preity will not hesitate to bite in. 'Elco at Hill Road, Bandra, is really clean. When I first went there, I made sure I took the owner's number and told him "you watch out, because if anything happens to me I am coming for you!"'

She is also a fan of Italian cuisine. 'When stranded in meat-eating countries, I reach out to simple Italian dishes – I'm rather fond of arrabiata and pomodoro sauces, and a crispy caesar salad. I like fish but not the creepy-crawly type! The fish at Nobu is wonderful, especially the black cod. They make the world's best black cod' Like a true Indian, Preity hates wasting food. 'I wish Hard Rock Café would serve smaller portions, something like small, medium and large so that people like me would not waste so much food!'

Preity enjoys food and learnt to cook in her home economics classes at school. She still loves pakoda kadhi and lemon rice, one of the first dishes she learnt to make. 'I love chatpat (tangy, spicy) stuff and have to go to Elco for that. I also prefer Indian-Chinese cuisine to authentic Chinese.' Growing up in Shimla on northern Indian dishes, she recalls a few unusual ones like a fern called lingda, sidku, a flower that is stuffed and steamed, and afeemdana ki roti (opium seed roti) which warms you up on cold winter days. She loves cooking for friends and family and experiments with flavours and spices. 'I even love to cook for my dogs (a boxer and an English bulldog) on their birthdays! It's just that there is little time now for that what with work commitments. But I do love cooking. I love putting cheese in everything.' Her dimples dance on her face as she recalls the fun she has with food.

above: Preity Zinta's most exciting film coming up is *Kabhi Alvida Na Kehna* where she is pitted against Rani Mukerji in a stellar cast of actors that only Karan Johar can bring together.

opposite page: Preity Zinta with Saif Ali Khan as they dance together in *Kal Ho Naa Ho* (2003). The film was directed by Nikhil Advani.

Bharwaan Gucchi

STUFFED MORELS

1¼lbs morels (gucchi)

FOR THE MARINADE
1¼ cups yogurt, hung in cheesecloth
    for 4 hours
¾ cup cream cheese
⅔ cup light cream
1½oz ground green cardamom seeds
1 teaspoon ground white pepper
salt to taste

FOR THE STUFFING
⅛ cup ghee (see page 155)
1½ onions, sliced and browned in a
    little ghee
11oz button mushrooms, boiled in
    a little water for 1 minute
1 large potato, boiled
¾ cup cottage cheese
1 tablespoon yellow chili powder
1 tablespoon ground cumin
2oz roasted ground channa dal
1 teaspoon turmeric
4 green chiles, seeded and
    finely chopped
2 tablespoons cilantro leaves, chopped
1 tablespoon ginger paste (see page 155)
2 teaspoons garam masala
    (see page 154)
salt to taste

serves 6

Morels are highly prized wild mushrooms. This recipe is a marvellous creation by chef Jitendra Kumar of the Masala Bay Restaurant at The Taj Lands End, a restaurant Preity Zinta likes to frequent for good Indian cuisine. Yellow chili powder is made from the second-grade red chiles that fade too much during the drying process, and sometimes a little turmeric is added. Use regular red chili powder if yellow is difficult to find.

Soak the morels in warm water for 10 minutes and drain, rinsing to make sure all the dirt is removed.

Heat the ghee for the stuffing in a large saucepan and add the stuffing ingredients one by one, stirring until they are well mixed. Set aside to cool.

Mix together the ingredients for the marinade.

Fill the morels with the stuffing and cover them with marinade. Set aside for about 30 minutes.

Thread the mushrooms onto 6 skewers and place on a barbecue or under a hot grill for 10 minutes, turning once. If you have a tandoor, this would be perfect.

Serve hot. Chutneys such as Green Mint and Cilantro or Tomato are ideal accompaniments.

Rajma

KIDNEY BEANS IN TOMATO SAUCE

1½ cups kidney beans, soaked overnight in 2 cups water

2 cinnamon sticks

2in piece of fresh ginger root, peeled and ground to a pulp

4 tablespoons vegetable oil

6 large onions, finely chopped

6 garlic cloves, sliced in half lengthways

4 green chiles, slit in half lengthways

8 large tomatoes, skinned and chopped

1 tablespoon red chili powder

2 tablespoons ground coriander

1 teaspoon turmeric

2 tablespoons garam masala (see page 154)

2 bay leaves

a large handful of cilantro leaves, chopped

salt to taste

serves 6

Drain and wash the kidney beans in running water.

Put the beans in a heavy saucepan, add the cinnamon, ginger, and some salt and cover with about 4 cups of water. Bring to a boil then reduce the heat and simmer for 50–60 minutes until the beans are just soft. (This can depend on the age of the beans.) Set aside to cool in their water.

In another saucepan, heat the oil and sauté the onions, garlic, and green chiles until the onions are light brown. Add the tomatoes and the red chili powder, ground coriander, turmeric, and garam masala, together with the bay leaves. Stir to prevent burning and cook for a few minutes until well blended.

Add the cooked kidney beans with the residual water into the masala mix and boil gently for 5 minutes.

Garnish with the cilantro and serve hot, with rice or roti.

Kaali Dal

CREAMY BLACK LENTILS

½ cup black lentils (urad dal), soaked overnight

2in piece of fresh ginger root, peeled and cut into julienne strips

2 green chiles, slit in half lengthways

1 tablespoon garlic paste (see page 155)

2 tablespoons sunflower oil

3 onions, thinly sliced

4 large tomatoes, skinned and cubed

serves 6

2 tablespoons ground coriander

1 teaspoon ground cumin seeds

½ teaspoon red chili powder

3½ tablespoons heavy cream

2 tablespoons ghee (see page 155)

½ teaspoon asafoetida powder

1 tablespoon garam masala (see page 154)

large handful of cilantro, chopped

salt to taste

This dal is at the heart of Punjabi cooking. In the old days it was put on to cook in the night and would be ready by morning on a dying coal fire. This modern recipe is as close as it gets.

Put the soaked dal in a saucepan with some salt, the ginger, green chiles, and garlic paste. Bring to a boil, stir and reduce the heat then simmer, covered, for about 50 minutes until the lentils are just soft.

In a separate large saucepan, heat the oil. Fry the onions until golden brown and then add the tomatoes. Stir-fry so that the tomatoes blend with the onions. Add the ground coriander, cumin, and red chili powder.

Add the cooked lentils to the onion-tomato masala and simmer for 10 minutes. Pour in the cream, stirring all the time. The lentils will now be thick and smooth in consistency.

In a small skillet, heat the ghee and add the asafoetida and garam masala. Stir for 1 minute and then pour over the cooked lentils and garnish with the chopped cilantro.

Serve hot, with tandoori rotis or naan.

Punjabi Pakoda Kadhi

CREAMY DUMPLING CURRY

FOR THE KADHI SAUCE
2 tablespoons gram flour
2 cups sour yogurt
1 teaspoon turmeric
1 tablespoon ground coriander
salt to taste

FOR THE PAKODAS
4oz gram flour
1 tablespoon red chili powder
1 teaspoon cumin seeds
½ teaspoon asafoetida powder
1 tablespoon fennel seeds, roasted
   and ground
1 large onion, finely chopped
3 green chiles, seeded and chopped
1 tablespoon dried pomegranate seeds
a large handful of cilantro leaves,
   chopped
pinch of baking soda
salt to taste

sunflower oil for deep frying

FOR THE TEMPERING
2 tablespoons ghee (see page 155)
pinch of asafoetida powder
2 whole red chiles
3 garlic cloves, sliced vertically
1 tablespoon black mustard seeds
1 green chile, seeded and slit
   lengthways
1 tablespoon ground coriander

serves 6

Preity adores home-style Punjabi food and this tops her favorites. This was one of the first dishes she was taught in her home economic lessons, and she recalls the recipe with a hint of nostalgia.

To make the Khadi sauce, mix the gram flour with a little water in a bowl to make a smooth paste. Add the yogurt, turmeric, and ground coriander and pour in 4 cups of water. Stir well and tip into a heavy saucepan. Bring to a boil then simmer, uncovered, for 30 minutes on a low heat. The water will reduce by half, leaving a thick kadhi.

Next, to make the pakodas put the gram flour into a bowl and mix in the chili powder, cumin, asafoetida, and fennel seeds. Stir in ¼ cup of water to make a thick paste, then add the onion, chiles, pomegranate seeds, cilantro, and baking soda and mix well. The pakoda batter should have a thick porridge-like texture.

Heat the oil in a large skillet and drop teaspoonfuls of the pakoda batter into the hot oil. Make sure the oil is sufficiently hot and smoking otherwise the dumplings tend to stick to the bottom of the pan. As they turn light brown, turn them with a ladle and, when browned on both sides, remove them and drain on paper towels. Dipping them into a bowl of cold water for a second or two helps to soften them a little.

Add the pakodas to the kadhi and cook for a few minutes.

Finally, in a small skillet, heat the ghee, add the tempering ingredients one by one and, once they all get crackling, pour the tempering over the kadhi, giving it a colorful garnish.

Serve hot, with boiled or fried basmati rice and papads.

BUTTER CHICKEN

2lbs skinned and boneless chicken,
   cut into 2in cubes
3½ tablespoons vegetable oil
3 onions, finely chopped
2 teaspoons ginger-garlic paste
   (see page 155)
2 cups chicken broth
15 almonds, soaked and ground
   to a paste
4 tablespoons butter
3 tablespoons light cream
a large handful of cilantro leaves

FOR THE MARINADE
juice of 1 lemon
1¼ cups yogurt
1 tablespoon garam masala
   (see page 154)
2 teaspoons red chili powder
1 tablespoon ground coriander
1 teaspoon ground cumin seeds
1 teaspoon dried fenugreek leaves,
   ground
salt to taste

FOR THE DRY SPICE MIX
6 cloves
10 black peppercorns
small cinnamon stick
1 teaspoon green cardamom seeds
2 bay leaves

serves 6

This dish, born somewhere among the highway dhabas of Punjab, is so popular that it made it to the title of a book—*Butter Chicken in Ludhiana*. It is the Indian counterpart of the chicken tikka masala, since both use tandoori-style chicken in a curry. In restaurants the chicken pieces always come from the tandoor but the recipe given below is for home-style preparation. To get the authentic smoky chicken flavor, replace the fried marinated chicken with tandoori chicken.

Mix all the marinade ingredients together in a large bowl. Add the chicken and stir to coat well, then marinate for 1 hour.

Meanwhile, dry-roast the ingredients for the dry spice mix and grind to a coarse powder. Set aside.

In a large saucepan, heat the oil and fry the onions and ginger-garlic paste to a golden brown. Add the marinated chicken pieces, leaving the yogurt-spice marinade aside. Fry the chicken until it turns opaque.

Add the dry spice mix and the chicken broth and cook until the chicken is tender—about 30 minutes. Stir in the yogurt-spice marinade. Bring to a boil slowly. When boiling, add the almond paste, butter, and cream and reduce the heat to low. Stir for a few minutes and garnish with cilantro leaves.

Serve hot, with tandoori roti or naan. Kaali Dal (see page 150) is a popular accompaniment.

ESSENTIALS

SPICES

SAMBHAR MASALA
Keeps for up to 6 months in a dry, airtight jar.

FOR TEN TABLESPOONS:
6 dried red chiles, seeds removed
2 cinnamon sticks
3 bay leaves
2 tablespoons cumin seeds
2 tablespoons coriander seeds
1 tablespoon cardamom seeds
1 tablespoon black mustard seeds
½ tablespoon mace
½ tablespoon cloves
½ tablespoon turmeric powder

Dry roast the ingredients except the turmeric. Cool, and grind them with the turmeric to a powder.

GARAM MASALA
Should be freshy made.

FOR TEN TABLESPOONS:
seeds from 10 green cardamoms
1 cinnamon stick
5 cloves
2 tablespoons black peppercorns
1 tablespoon cumin seeds
2 tablespoons coriander seeds
1 teaspoon grated nutmeg

Dry roast the ingredients except the nutmeg. Cool, and grind them with the nutmeg into a powder.

BHATTI MASALA
Keeps for up to 6 months in a dry, airtight jar

¼oz each of whole coriander seeds, black peppercorns, cumin seeds, dried fenugreek leaves, cinnamon powder, red chili powder, cloves, cardamoms, nutmeg, and mace

Grind the spices together.

AWADHI MASALA
Should be freshy made.

FOR TWO TABLESPOONS:
1 tablespoon mace powder
1 tablespoon nutmeg powder

Mix and use.

DHANSAK MASALA
Keeps for up to 6 months in a dry, airtight jar.

FOR TEN TABLESPOONS:
6 red chiles, seeds removed
1 cinnamon stick, about 3in long
3 bay leaves
2 tablespoons cumin seeds
2 tablespoons coriander seeds
seeds of 6 cardamoms (green or black)
2 tablespoons black peppercorns
5 cloves
1 tablespoon fenugreek seeds
1 tablespoon black mustard seeds
½ tablespoon turmeric
½ tablespoon mace

Dry roast the ingredients except the turmeric for 1 minute until the aroma leaves the spices. Cool, add the turmeric and grind to a powder.

PAO BHAJI MASALA

½ teaspoon cumin seeds
1½ teaspoons red chili powder
2 teaspoons ground coriander
¼ teaspoon turmeric
1 teaspoon garam masala
1 teaspoon green mango powder (amchoor)
5 cloves
pinch of asafoetida
pinch of black salt powder
salt to taste

Toast cumin seeds and grind to a powder with the cloves. Then stir all the spices together.

TANDOORI CHAT MASALA

FOR TEN TABLESPOONS:
1 tablespoon black pepper
1 tablespoon cumin seeds, roasted and ground
1 tablespoon black salt powder
½oz dried mint leaves, crushed
¼oz dried fenugreek leaves, ground
2 tablespoons green mango powder (amchoor)
1 tablespoon green cardamom seeds, roasted and ground
1 tablespoon cloves, ground
½ tablespoon ginger powder
½ tablespoon mace powder
1 tablespoon red chili powder
pinch of asafoetida powder

Mix and use.

PARATHAS

Paratha is a generic name for a wide range of breads made in north India, from plain parathas to stuffed ones. Ajowan is widely available in specialty Indian stores—it is also known as bishop's weed, carom, or omum.

BASIC PARATHA

MAKES 12 PARATHAS:
1 tablespoon ajowan
1 teaspoon salt
4 cups whole-wheat flour (atta or chapatti flour)
3oz ghee (see page 155)

Mix the salt and ajowan evenly into the flour. Make a well in the center of the flour and mix about 1–1¼ cups of water, a little at a time, into the flour to make an elastic dough. Knead until the dough is well blended and smooth. Rest it for a few minutes, then divide it into 12 equal sized portions.

Parathas are rolled in different directions to give the layered effect. The simplest way is to roll out each portion onto a floured work surface. Spread half a teaspoon of ghee on

the top. Then fold in half and repeat again so it takes the shape of a triangle. Roll out again, using flour to dust when necessary, to form a 6x4in triangle.

Heat a heavy skillet and place a paratha on it. Turn on both sides, dabbing with a little ghee each time. Keep turning and moving it gently with a flat spoon or spatula until golden brown. After 2 turns on each side you should have an aromatic paratha, crisp on the outside and soft on the inside.

Serve hot with butter and yogurt.

STUFFED PARATHAS

There is a wide range of stuffings for parathas, spicy potatoes are a classic. Almost any vegetable works, as long as the stuffing is dry. The recipe for the basic paratha dough remains the same.

SPICY POTATO STUFFING

12 boiled potatoes
1 tablespoon red chili powder
1 tablespoon green mango powder (amchoor)
small bunch of cilantro, finely chopped
2 green chiles, finely chopped
salt to taste

Mash the potatoes and add the chili powder, mango powder, and salt. Mix evenly with the cilantro and green chiles. Separate into 12 portions.

Roll out the portions of dough to form rounds about 6–7in in diameter. Place a portion of the stuffing in the center. Gather the edges of the disc to the center and close them tightly leaving no gaps. Roll out again, using flour to dust when necessary, to the same sized rounds. Cook as above.

OTHER STUFFINGS

For all but the onion stuffing, substitute the suggested stuffing for the potatoes in the above method:

Paneer
Peas—lightly cooked and mashed
Cauliflower—use raw shredded cauliflower
Radishes—shred finely and squeeze out the water
Onions—finely chop the onions and add while making the dough, then follow the basic paratha method

ROTIS OR CHAPATTIS

Also referred to as phulka, this bread is the staple all over north and central India, with the exception of Kashmir. Made on an iron griddle called a tava, it is always served hot. A flat wooden or marble base and rolling pin are used to roll out rotis.

MAKES 18 CHAPATTIS/ROTIS:
4 cups whole-wheat flour (atta or chapatti flour)

Make the dough (leaving 4 tablespoonfuls of flour aside) adding 1–1¼ cups of water, a little at a time to ensure an even mix and smooth, firm dough. Water quantities vary according to the kind of wheat flour, so use the water with care.

Leave to rest for 10 minutes and then divide into 18 equal portions.

Take each portion between your hands and roll to form a round ball. Use the reserved flour to dust and with a rolling pin make a thin, round, flat sheet. This takes a little practice. The trick is to move the ball of dough in a manner in which all sides get evenly rolled.

On a hot griddle, dry-roast the roti, ensuring that it is turned over just as it begins to cooks. The heat creates steam within the dough so it rises and fluffs up, creating a soft and perfect roti.

Rotis are often eaten plain but many traditionally serve them with a bit of ghee or butter brushed on one side.

BASIC RECIPES

PURE GHEE

In India ghee is made from vegetable oils or butter. Pure ghee is made from unsalted butter—it is clarified butter from which the excess moisture has been removed. Where pure ghee is called for, make sure it is a milk-based ghee. Ghee can be bought in Indian stores or made easily using the following recipe:

Melt butter in a heavy saucepan over low heat. Turn up the heat and bring to a boil, until the butter is foaming. Turn the heat to very low and simmer, uncovered and without stirring, for 45 minutes; the milk solids at the bottom of the pan will turn golden in color and the liquid at the top will be transparent.

Remove from the heat and strain the butter through a strainer lined with a good-quality cheesecloth; you may have to do this several times until the ghee is absolutely clear. Pour into glass jars and seal tightly. This keeps well for months if no moisture is allowed to get into the jar.

GARLIC PASTE
Peel garlic cloves and blend in a food-processor for 10 seconds.

GINGER PASTE
Peel ginger and roughly chop it, then blend it in a food-processor until very coarsely ground.

GARLIC–GINGER PASTE
Mix equal quantities of peeled garlic and ginger and blend to make the paste in a food-processor. Add a little water if necessary.

Garlic-ginger paste can be made up in batches and frozen. Make sure it is in well-sealed plastic bags or everything else in the freezer will take on the aroma!

UNSPOOLING BOLLYWOOD:

Classic Moments from the Indian Film Industry

Indians took to films very quickly—within years of the first Lumiere films in Mumbai they were being shown all over India. The first feature film was produced in 1913 and through famine, economic depression, and the two world wars Bollywood continued to seduce people from all walks of life with their promise of escape and fantasy. The migration of talent to Mumbai, the city of dreams, continues unabated even today—Bollywood Fever is set to become a global epidemic.

left: Alam Ara
Silent films were made in India from 1899. The first feature film was *Raja Harishchandra* in 1913. By the late 1920s, the industry was producing over twenty-five films a year. *Alam Ara* (1931) was India's first non-silent film with seven songs and dialogues in Hindustani (a mix of Hindi and Urdu languages). It was a big hit and spawned a tradition of musical films that endures today. One film from this period, *Indrasabha*, included seventy-one songs! Almost all regional cinemas in India released non-silent films in that year.

opposite page: Navrang
The 1940s belonged to the film director V. Shantaram. He had a cinematic style that was innovative and courageous and he understood the role of film as a social commentary. His black and white photography was imaginative and his storytelling poignant. His musical sensibilities were special—he would not use background music and created lush song sequences in many of his films.

राजकमल का रंगीन चित्र
नवरंग
SANDHYA
in
NAVRANG
DIRECTED BY
V. SHANTARAM
COLOR BY
TECHNICOLOR
نورنگ
ORIENTAL OFFSET & LITHO WORKS, BOMBAY. 7.

MEHBOOB PRODUCTIONS PRIVATE LTD. PRESENT
NARGIS · SUNIL DUTT · RAJENDRA KUMAR & RAAJ KUMAR
MOTHER INDIA
TECHNICOLOR
मदर इंडिया
مدر انڈیا
DIRECTED BY
MEHBOOB
MUSIC
NAUSHAD

opposite page: Mother India
Mother India (1957) is an epic film centered on the strength of Indian women, and it received an Oscar nomination. It was a remake of Mehboob Khan's earlier film *Aurat* (Woman), in which he personified the Indian nation as a woman.

above: Awara
By the 1950s, the golden period of Indian filmmaking set in with confident young filmmakers like Raj Kapoor, Bimal Roy, Guru Dutt, and Mehboob Khan shaping the form and style of films. India was celebrating its newly won independence, and these young filmmakers displayed highly personal styles and a strong commitment to positive socialism.

Don

The 1970s are marked by the "angry young man" image created by screenwriters Salim-Javed in numerous films, most notably *Zanjeer* (1973) and *Deewar* (1975), and portrayed so famously by Amitabh Bachchan. The political environment of the Emergency and its lifting, created an inherent anger within the consciousness of the people and this was expressed through the medium of film. Chandra Barot's *Don* (1977), with Amitabh Bachchan as the Don, defined Bollywood's stylization with such flair that it is being remade as a big-budget film starring Shah Rukh Khan.

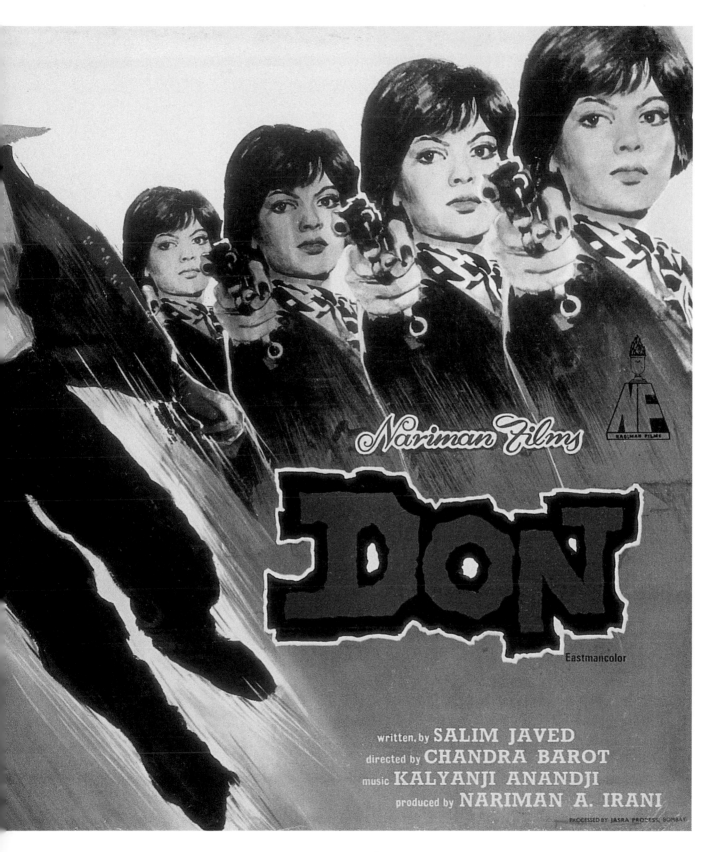

Raj Kapoor's

SANGAM

TECHNICOLOR

left: Sangam

Sangam (1964) is one of Raj Kapoor's more flamboyant films. Shot in color in five European locations (very unusual and extravagant at this time), the film was a big hit and set the tone for romantic musicals shot in exotic locations that are still popular today. With the innovation of color, filmmakers found a youthful energy and a lot of the films of the 1960s carried a vivacious sense of fashion, interiors, and musical rhythms that had clear Western influences.

right: Sahib Bibi Aur Ghulam

At the end of the black and white period of the early 1960s, *Sahib Bibi Aur Ghulam* (1962) was released. This hauntingly beautiful film is set in the dying days of the zamindars (wealthy landlords) of Bengal. Seen through the eyes of a simple villager who comes to work in a haveli (mansion), the decadence and languishing moral world of the wealthy is touchingly portrayed by Meena Kumari and Rehmaan. Subtle acting, achingly poetic songs, and wonderful camerawork make it a memorable film.

opposite page: Guide

Dev Anand and his brother Vijay Anand brought modernity to Indian cinema. *Guide* (1965) was based on R.K. Narayan's novel and made in both English and Hindi. It depicted a married woman's search for love and freedom through a friendship with a tour guide who is devastated when she leaves to pursue a successful career. The songs and dance sequences showed originality and became a touchstone for films to come.

DEV ANAND
WAHEEDA REHMAN
Nav Ketan International's
guide
EASTMANCOLOR
PROCESSED & PRINTED IN NEW YORK
DIRECTED BY
VIJAY ANAND
MUSIC
S. D. BURMAN

Mughal-e-Azam
A huge historical film that took fifteen years to complete, making it the most expensive film ever made. Set in the court of Mughal emperor Akbar, *Mughal-e-Azam* tells the tale of the love between his son Prince Salim and court dancer Anarkali. The film is a cinematographic delight—shot in black and white, it used color film for the song sequence "Jab Pyaar Kiya To Darna Kya," where the gorgeous Madhubala dances and is reflected in thousands of mirrors. First released in 1960, the entire film was retouched in color and re-released in 2004.

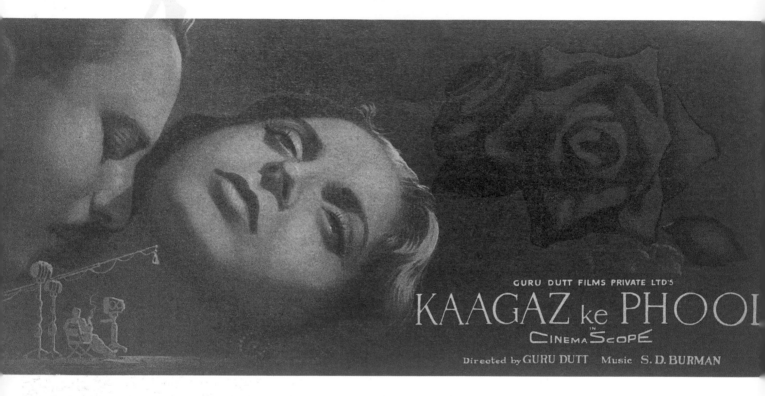

above: Kaagaz Ke Phool

The late 1950s classic, *Kaagaz Ke Phool* is full of pathos and memorable songs. It is the story of a film director looking back through the ruins of his film studio and remembering his successful and passionate years of film making. The film has incredible lighting and mood created by V. K. Murthy and it is also India's first Cinemascope film. Guru Dutt, its director, also played the lead role and the film's failure at the box office effected him deeply, propelling him on a downward spiral to suicide.

opposite page: Pakeezah

Hindi films have always been preoccupied with the Mughal period due to its rich heritage of poetry and defined cultural stylistic sense. Of the many films made against the backdrop of the Mughal period, *Pakeezah*, made in the early 1970s, became iconic. Meera Kumari and Kamaal Amrohi, the director of the movie and her husband, created an alluring tale told tastefully with a great musical score. Her death soon after the release of the film turned it into an instant classic.

SIPPY FILMS PRESENT
JAYA BHADURI

WRITTEN BY   MUSIC
SALIM JAVED • R.D.BURMAN
LYRICS   CAMERA
ANAND BAKSHI • DWARKA DIVECHA

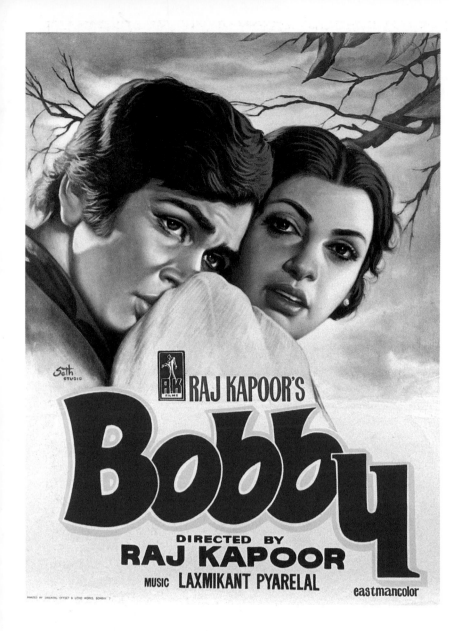

opposite page: Umrao Jaan
The glamorous diva Rekha immortalized the courtesan culture of Lucknow and Kanpur in *Umrao Jaan* (1981). With its impeccable poetry, costumes, and Muslim esthetics, the film is lovingly indulgent to the period it represents. The ghazals (poetic songs) of the film have become immortal and though the film is being currently remade, it remains to be seen if it will match the achievements of the original.

previous page: Sholay
Sholay (1975) made film history and broke records at the box office. It has become so iconic that its dialogues are seeped in the national consciousness. In this revenge saga, directed by Ramesh Sippy, the biggest stars came together to create the kind of magic that is impossible to repeat. Amitabh Bachchan was a rising star at this point and his superstar and legendary status were still to come. With a great story full of surprises and punches, it also marks the high point for the screenwriting duo Salim-Javed.

above: Bobby
Bobby (1973) set the trend for teenage romances that continue to be popular today. Raj Kapoor made this film after the failure of *Mera Naam Joker* (1970). He recreated the magic of his films from the 1940s and '50s when he starred opposite Nargis, by casting his teenage son Rishi Kapoor opposite a young Dimple Kapadia, who even looked a bit like Nargis. The film was a smash hit and its funky clothes and accessories were copied by teenagers all over the country.

Music: Khayyam   Lyrics: Shahryar   A film by Muzaffar Ali

BEST OF BOLLYWOOD:
1995-2006

Note sequence: Film; year; director; stars; producer

Dilwale Dulhaniya Le Jayenge;
1995; Aditya Chopra; Shah Rukh Khan, Kajol;
Yashraj films

Rangeela;
1995; Ram Gopal Varma; Aamir Khan, Urmilla
Matondkar, Jackie Shroff; Ram Gopal Varma

Karan Arjun;
1995; Rakesh Roshan; Shah Rukh Khan, Kajol;
Rakesh Roshan

Khamoshi—The Musical;
1996; Sanjay Leela Bhansali; Manisha Koirala,
Salman Khan, Nana Patekar; Sibte Hassan Rizvi

Dil To Pagal Hai;
1997; Yash Chopra; Madhuri Dixit, Shah Rukh
Khan, Karisma Kapoor; Yash Chopra

Pardes;
1997; Subhash Ghai; Shah Rukh Khan, Mahima
Chowdhury; Mukta Arts

Kuch Kuch Hota Hai;
1998; Karan Johar; Shah Rukh Khan, Kajol, Rani
Mukerji; Dharma Productions

Chachi 420;
1998; Kamalahasan; Tabu, Amrish Puri;
Kamalahasan

Satya;
1998; Ram Gopal Varma; J.D.Chakravarti, Urmila
Matondkar; Ram Gopal Varma

Dil Se;
1998; Mani Ratnam; Shah Rukh Khan, Manisha
Koirala; Jhamu Sugandh

Ghulam;
1998; Vikram Bhatt; Aamir Khan, Rani Mukerji;
Mukesh Bhatt

Hum Dil De Chuke Sanam;
1999; Sanjay Leela Bhansali; Salman Khan,
Aishwarya Rai, Ajay Devgun; Jhamu Sugandh

Taal;
1999; Subhash Ghai; Aishwarya Rai, Anil Kapoor,
Akshay Khanna; Mukta Arts

Mohabbatein;
2000; Aditya Chopra; Amitabh Bachchan, Shah
Rukh Khan, Aishwarya Rai; Yashraj Flms

Kaho Na Pyaar Hai;
2000; Rakesh Roshan; Hrithik Roshan, Amisha
Patel; Rakesh Roshan

Kabhi Khushi Kabhie Gham;
2001; Karan Johar; Shah Rukh Khan, Kajol, Hrithik
Roshan, Kareena Kapoor, Amitabh Bachchan;
Dharma Productions

Lagaan;
2001; Ashutosh Gowarikar; Aamir Khan, Gracy
Singh; Aamir Khan

Dil Chahta Hai;
2001; Farhaan Akhtar; Aamir Khan, Priety Zinta,
Saif Ali Khan; Ritesh Sidhwani

Saathiya;
2002; Shaad Ali; Rani Mukerji, Vivek Oberoi;
Mani Ratnam

Devdas;
2002; Sanjay Leela Bhansali; Shah Rukh Khan,
Aishwarya Rai, Madhuri Dixit; Bharat Shah

Munnabhai M.B.B.S;
2003; Rajkumar Hirani; Sanjay Dutt, Gracy Singh, Arshad Warsi; Vidhu Vinod Chopra

Kal Ho Naa Ho;
2003; Nikhil Advani; Shah Rukh Khan, Preity Zinta, Saif Ali Khan; Karan Johar

Koi Mil Gaya;
2003; Rakesh Roshan; Hrithik Roshan, Preity Zinta; Rakesh Roshan

Chalte Chalte;
2003; Aziz Mirza; Shah Rukh Khan, Rani Mukerji; Dreamz Unlimited

Hum Tum;
2004; Kunal Kohli; Saif Ali Khan, Rani Mukerji; Yashraj Films

Veer Zaara;
2004; Yash Chopra; Shah Rukh Khan, Preity Zinta, Rani Mukerji; Yashraj Films

Main Hoon Na;
2004; Farah Khan; Shah Rukh Khan, Sushmita Sen, Sunil Shetty; Dreamz Unlimited

Swades;
2004; Ashutosh Gowarikar; Shah Rukh Khan, Kishori Ballal, Gayatri Sinha, Makarand Deshpande; Ashutosh Gowarikar

Yuva;
2004; Mani Ratnam; Abhishek Bachchan, Rani Mukerji; Mani Ratnam

Dhoom;
2004; Sanjay Gadhvi; Abhishek Bachchan, John Abraham, Esha Deol; Aditya Chopra

Bunty Aur Babli;
2005; Shaad Ali; Amitabh Bachchan, Abhishek Bachchan, Rani Mukerjee; Yashraj Films

Salaam Namaste;
2005; Siddharta Anand; Saif Ali Khan, Preity Zinta; Yashraj films

Parineeta;
2005; Pradeep Sarkar; Saif Ali Khan, Vidya Balan, Sanjay Dutt; Vidhu Vinod Chopra

Iqbal;
2005; Nagesh Kukunoor; Nasseruddin Shah, Shreyas Talpade; Subhash Ghai

Black;
2005; Sanjay Leela Bhansali; Rani Mukerji, Amitabh Bachchan; Sanjay Leela Bhansali

The Rising: Mangal Pandey;
2005; Ketan Mehta; Aamir Khan, Rani Mukerji; Bobby Bedi

Rang De Basanti;
2006; Rakeysh Mehra; Aamir Khan, Soha Ali Khan; Rakeysh Mehra

Taxi 9211;
2006; Milan Luthria; Nana Patekar, John Abrahim; Ramesh Sippy

INDEX

RESTAURANTS

(Listed in alphabetical order)

Aap Ki Khatir (Kebabs)
Opposite Humayun's Tomb
Nizzamuddin East
New Delhi 110013
(a small roadside eatery)

Bauji Ka Dhaba (Indian)
Hauz Khas Village
New Delhi 110016
T: 91 11 26525511/26512324
&
Metropolitan Mall
Gurgaon V 122015
T: 91 1232 24410167

China Garden (Chinese)
Crossroads
Tardeo, Haji Ali
Mumbai 400034
T: 91 22 24955588/24955589

Elco's (Snacks)
Hill Road
Bandra West
Mumbai 400050
T: 91 22 26437206/26457677/
9820129075

**Gazalee Coastal Food
(Seafood)**
Kadamgiri Complex
Hanuman Road
Vile Parle East
Mumbai 400057
T: 91 22 28388093/28226470

Indigo (Fusion)
4 Mandlik Rd
Off Colaba Causeway
Mumbai 400005
T: 91 22 5636 8999

**Mahesh Lunch Home (Malwani
Seafood)**
8 D, Cavasji Patel Street,
Fort, Mumbai 400001
T: 91 22 22870938/22023965

Mangi Ferra (Italian)
7 Gulmohar Cross Road
JVPD Scheme
Juhu
Mumbai 400049
T: 91 22 56751728/9

**Masala Bay (Indian) & Ming
Yang (Chinese)**
Taj Land's End
Bandstand
Bandra West
Mumbai 400050
T: 91 22 66011825

New Yorker (Iranian)
25 Chowpatty Seaface
Mumbai 400007
T: 91 22 23643232

Olive Bar and Kitchen (Fusion)
14, Union Park
Khar
Mumbai 400050
T: 91 22 2600 8248

Pan Asian
Marriot Welcom Hotel
District Centre Saket
New Delhi 110017
T: 91 11 2652 1122

Royal China (Chinese)
Behind Sterling Movie Theatre
Hazarimal Somani Marg
Fort, Mumbai 400001
T: 91 22 5635 5310/1

Sagar (South Indian)
18 Defence Colony Market
New Delhi 110024
T: 91 11 24678374/24617832

Saltwater Grill
H20 Water Sports Complex
Next to Mafatlal Swimming Club
Marine Drive
Mumbai 400007
T: 91 22 23685459

Sarvi (North Indian)
186/190
Nagpada
Mumbai 400003
T: 91 22 23095989

**Thai Pavilion (Thai)/
Konkan Café (Coastal)/
Trattoria (Italian)**
Taj President
Cuffe Parade
Mumbai 400 005
T: 91 22 6665 0808

Tiffin
The Oberoi
Nariman Point
Mumbai 400021
T: 91 22 6632 5757

Trishna (Seafood)
Saibaba Marg, next to Commerce
House
Kala Ghoda,
Fort, Mumbai 400023
T: 91 22 22672176

Urban Tadka (Indian)
Seven Bungalows
Andheri West
Mumbai 400061
T: 91 22 56028943

**Wasabe by Morimoto
(Japanese)**
The Taj Mahal Palace & Tower
Apollo Bunder
Mumbai 400001
T: 91 22 66653366